Lessons in Life

Andria Zafirakou is a Vice Principal at the Swiss Cottage School, Research and Development Centre. Her specialist subjects are arts and textiles and for the last nineteen years she has worked in some of the most marginalised communities in London. She has been acknowledged internationally as an education leader, receiving numerous accolades, including: the million-dollar Global Teacher Prize in 2018, being recognised as a Culture Leader by the World Economic Forum, a Thought Leader for the OECD and a Member of the High-Level Panel on the Teaching Profession, which was established by the UN Secretary-General in 2023. She has an Honorary Doctorate from the University of Worcester and was honoured by the late Queen Elizabeth II with an MBE for her services to education. Her first book, *Those Who Can, Teach*, was published by Bloomsbury in 2021.

Lessons in Life

What we can all learn from
the world's best teachers

Andria Zafirakou

QUERCUS

First published in Great Britain in 2023 by Quercus Editions Ltd
This paperback published in 2024 by

QUERCUS

Quercus Editions Ltd
Carmelite House
50 Victoria Embankment
London EC4Y 0DZ

An Hachette UK company

A CIP catalogue record for this book is available
from the British Library.

PB ISBN 978 152942 234 4
Ebook ISBN 978 1 52942 232 0

10 9 8 7 6 5 4 3 2 1

Typeset by CC Book Production
Printed and bound in Great Britain by Clays Ltd, Elcograf S.p.A.

Papers used by Quercus are from well-managed forests and other responsible sources.

To all teachers everywhere.

Introduction

If I were to ask you which person changed your life, it's likely the first person you thought of would be a teacher. I know this because I often start my public speaking events with the same question and see a room of hands go up in agreement. A selfless army of people – with the multifaceted role of educator, problem-solver, listener, creator, carer, leader, supporter and believer – teachers can make a positive lasting impact on young people, their families and the wider society. Long may we recognise, respect and celebrate them. Yet it works both ways. The best teachers are also those shaped by their students, who educate them on the most important lessons in life.

This is where the inspiration for this book comes from. I wanted to gather the voices of some of the very best educators in the world and ask them to share their stories of students who made a difference to them, professionally and personally. Not only are these lessons we learn as teachers, but they also help parents understand their children better and adults communicate with young people, whether in a home, social or work environment.

I was lucky to know exactly who to speak to when writing this book. In 2018, I won the Global Teacher Prize. Of the 33,000 nominations from 175 countries, I was presented with the annual award, given by the Varkey Foundation to an exceptional teacher who has made an outstanding contribution to their profession. It was a pivotal moment for me and it boosted my confidence in my ability. It was a humbling one too, giving me a greater insight into education globally and shining a light on some of our unsung teaching heroes. Through this award, and my twenty-year career, I have met the most amazing teachers, and I have invited thirty of them to take part in this project. I wanted to explore their experiences in the classroom and reveal the incredible truths they have discovered from working with young people.

Each of these teachers faces difficult challenges in the workplace, whether it's with the curriculum, cultural taboos, racism, absent or overprotective parents, mental health issues, corruption, girls' rights, generational trauma, knife crime, lack of funding or teaching in a war-torn country. Their unique accounts are at times heartbreaking, astounding, funny and painful, but are always inspiring, and it has been an absolute honour to talk to them and capture their voices here. We may not all speak the same language but we are united in our commitment to education and our students' wellbeing. I know I can walk into any school, in any tiny village, in any country, in any continent and I will feel at home.

As I have asked my colleagues to open up about the students who impacted them, it seems only right to start with one of my own and a boy who we shall call Alvaro. That isn't his real name, but we have changed the names of all the students who appear in this book to protect their identities. Alvaro joined our school at the end of Year 9, when he was fourteen. He had come from a special educational needs school and his parents wanted him to have a mainstream education resulting in GCSE exams, but had no expectation of him passing any. Alvaro was selectively mute, with learning challenges, and refused to participate in my art class. As a young teacher, I thought I could make a difference, but after a few lessons I was stumped. I could see how traumatised he was by the school environment and I was struggling to communicate with him. I had no idea how to progress.

A couple of weeks later, at the end of another lesson when Alvaro had done nothing, I was chatting to a couple of students at the front of the class as everyone left. Out of the corner of my eye, I saw Alvaro put something on my desk and then run towards the door. I shouted for him to stop. On a sheet of lined paper, torn out of one of his class books, he had drawn the most astounding picture of a guitar I had ever seen. I was ecstatic. He could do it! More to the point, he wanted to do it! And I knew I could help him. I told him his work was outstanding and he just looked at me, his grey eyes full of surprise. I filled his school bag with art equipment and paper and told him to draw five things by the following week. He produced his work at the next lesson and I showed the rest of the class, who were genuinely pleased and congratulated him. Alvaro's confidence and pride in his work grew quickly. He and his parents were thrilled with the D grade he achieved in his GCSE. So was I, but I knew with more time he could do better. He stayed on for sixth form and took art and photography at A level, and scored A grades in both.

The most beautiful part of Alvaro's journey was not the qualifications, but how he changed as a person. He would often come into my classroom, sit at the back and get on with his own work. When the younger students were there they would chat to him and I would tell them off for being distracted, but secretly I was thrilled that he was conversing. Alvaro became a big part of the school community and even gained the confidence to perform in the school production. He had found his passion and, in the process, he taught me not to lower my expectations of students or take them at face value, but to give them time and space to show me who they are and what they can do.

Every day I learn something from my students, as we build a relationship and I track their journey through education. I was reminded of this again recently, with a student, Jacob, who had been struggling with art. I could not get him to engage and many of my colleagues were finding him difficult to teach. In my class, he would attempt the task set but, soon after, he would rip up his work and pronounce himself 'rubbish'. I could see his confidence and self-esteem diminishing and it was exhausting for both him and me. When we started a new project about identity, I thought this may be more challenging because it was so personal and I knew he would battle to engage. I didn't want him to feel under any pressure, I just wanted him to be emboldened by the subject matter and enjoy the process. He produced a piece of work that reminded me of the American artist Jean-Michel Basquiat. It was raw and brilliant. I showed him who Jean-Michel was on the computer and he was blown away by the comparison. He transformed from a kid I cajoled to come into the classroom to a focused, prolific artist. Jacob realised his work did count and that he was just as entitled to be there as the other students. Some young people feel so isolated and it can sometimes take a simple thing, or sometimes it takes a bigger eureka moment, to change this trajectory. As teachers, we don't know what can trigger this, but when it happens we must harness it.

I see this echoed in my colleagues' insightful reflections throughout this book. In the myriad ways they find to connect with their students, like Martin establishing a radio station in his Buenos Aires school, Scottish headteacher David involving his students in a regenerative community project or Armand turning his Canadian school into Hogwarts and running a week of Harry Potter-themed lessons. Not only does this style of teaching take a huge amount of energy, creativity and drive, it also requires courage to deviate from the traditional school structure and work outside of paid hours. Bravery is a central theme throughout, shown in pupils and teachers alike, including in Marjorie and Andrew's battles and Esther and Leticia's maverick approach. Howard and Swaroop remind parents to treat children as individuals and allow them to make their own choices. Peter talks of refusing to give up and Maggie tells of students who have made her a better person. Above all, every single one of them respects and believes in the children they teach.

What at first may seem like a guidebook for teachers is in fact a quest of courage, hope and love that reaches far beyond offering solutions in the classroom. It is a precious resource of strategies, ideas and thoughts for parents and adults who want to understand and communicate with the children in their lives. I sincerely hope that, for whatever reason you hold this book in your hands, you get what you need from it.

Andria Zafirakou\
43, London, UK

Nadia Lopez

45, New York, USA

'I'm a firm believer in providing children with experiences to prepare them for the world. Without the parameters that stop them exploring what it means to be autonomous'

As a student, Nadia had a phobia of maths. The subject made her anxious and she was unable to concentrate during lessons, but her teacher was oblivious to her difficulties. Yet, when Nadia graduated as a special education teacher, qualified to teach all subject areas, it was maths that fascinated her. She knew how it felt to struggle in the classroom and she wanted to help, not just the students, but the teachers who needed to know how to reach them. This set the tone for Nadia's twenty-year career as a teacher, principal, coach and mentor in Brooklyn, New York.

Special education often carries negative associations, highlighting students who struggle in different areas of learning and setting them apart from their seemingly more capable peers. Nadia witnessed this first-hand, both as a teacher – in education in America, special education was considered a place not a service – and with her students, who felt marginalised. They had been told they couldn't do anything. Nadia was determined to prove the system wrong.

'These young people would react and respond to others' labelling of them. They would act up because no one had taken the time to talk to them, to learn about them. Nobody had told them that they were exceptional, that they could learn in a different way and still show their tremendous talents. Because of my mission, I was considered the disrupter, hell-bent on doing the things that professionals in the industry said I couldn't do, or said that the children couldn't do.'

Getting students to recognise their own personal brilliance has been Nadia's biggest purpose and greatest accomplishment. She knows the odds were stacked against the children, many of whom came from Black, Latin and Bangladeshi communities, with more than 40 per cent of the families living below the poverty line. Some of the children she taught were also dealing with trauma and mental health issues stemming from abuse or living in shelters or having been forcibly placed into care. Nadia established a wraparound service to support these students and offered an extended day, with the school staying open until 6 p.m. from Monday to Saturday.

Nadia was acutely aware of the mixed feelings of parents towards her and the school. While they wanted the best for their children, her mission could at times bring to the fore their own inadequacies. They also harboured suspicions towards a system that had failed them as students. Their experience of school was an institution that didn't care about them. It took time for Nadia to build their trust, and she would regularly comfort and reassure parents.

'I would tell them I am not a threat and thank them for allowing me to have access to, what I consider, the most precious gifts that they could ever give to the world. It was also important to tell them that my parents were immigrants and the only thing they could give me of any worth was education.'

She would talk to them about their own educational journeys. Many of them had dropped out by the time they got into the same grade their children were in then. So the fact that their children were still there, and thriving, was a great achievement. She involved them in activities and encouraged them to volunteer on school trips. In some cases, she was teaching them things they themselves had not been taught as children. She recalls one of her students, Sasha, who came to her just after she graduated and asked Nadia for a favour. She said her mother couldn't read and she was worried about leaving her when she went to college as there was no one else to read for her. Nadia spoke to Sasha's old seventh-grade teacher, who said she would be happy to give one-to-one sessions.

'We called Sasha's mother into school and sat with her and her daughter. Sasha spoke movingly about how much time her mum had spent prioritising Sasha's education. She told her it was her turn now and that she wanted her to have the benefit of learning. It was wonderful to see this sixteen-year-old value her education and want to share the power of it with her mum. The lessons were a triumph and she learned to read.'

What Nadia created, first as a teacher and then as principal, was a community that defined what success looked like and celebrated that. It encouraged students to be serious about their learning and to hold each other accountable too. Over the years there have been many students who have stayed in Nadia's heart, like shy Nica, who she met in her third year of teaching. Nica had transitioned from the most restrictive special education class of twelve students, with one teacher and a support, to the next stage with the collaborative team of Nadia and another teacher.

'She had swag to her. You could tell by her clothes and sneakers; she dressed like the cool kid. But she never spoke. I would watch her in class and I knew she wanted to say something but she held back each time. One day there was some incident, so minor I can't remember what it was, and I was trying to sort it out, and I noticed Nica started to cry. I pulled her outside and asked her what was wrong. You know what she said to me? She said, "I have never been in a place where people care." She had never been taught by someone who cared so much.'

In her previous class, Nica had been the only girl and the teacher had found it impossible to control the class. Consequently, Nica spent most of the day fighting off the boys, who were either making inappropriate advances or ridiculing her. She spent her school days in a type of war zone so that there was little time to learn anything. In Nadia's class, the students were not allowed to make fun of anybody or touch them. And play-fighting, which usually led to proper blows, was banned. There were specific ground rules and Nadia enforced them.

'Nica said it was the first time she wasn't afraid to be in the classroom. Her mum said she wasn't sure what I did in class but she no longer had to force Nica to come to school. In fact, when she got home she would talk about her day and choose to read books. And at lunchtimes, Nica and her new friend, Stephanie, would give dance lessons to other girls. I saw this child blossom in front of me and it was a huge turning point in my career. I hadn't quite realised the depths of a child's school experience and how it can break or make their future. Nica developed agency for herself and she saw how she should be treated.'

Nadia believes, and I agree, that, without Nica moving classes and experiencing the difference between a teacher who cares and one who doesn't, she would have dropped out of school. It would have been too hard for her to continue to protect herself and focus on learning for her specific educational needs. So, what did happen to Nica?

'She did exceptionally well. I saw her a few years later and she was planning to go to City College and get a degree. I mean, that conversation got me. Those moments . . .'

It gives me goosebumps hearing this, and I can see why this was such a defining moment in Nadia's teaching journey. It showed her not only how important it was to watch her students closely, but also that a good relationship between teacher and student isn't assumed.

'It fascinates me that we spend a lot of time building relationships with other adults yet, when it comes to children, we want to speed up the process and expect them to be open with us when they don't know us. This doesn't happen between adults so why should it with children? We can't just expect them to be open with us without gaining their trust first.'

Nadia has developed ways to connect with even her most unreachable students. She has learned so much from them, about how and when to talk to them. If a student didn't want to speak Nadia would bring them to her office and turn the TV on or give them a book. She would also give them a piece of paper.

'The way my room was set up, I had artwork from the students, pictures of my family and sayings on the wall. It was reflective of who I was and, in this invitation to be in my space, I was saying that I trusted them. I would tell them I was going to get on with some work while they sat. And the piece of paper was for the moment when they felt ready to write down what was wrong. Or to let me know they were ready to talk. I never made them speak to me.'

There was one student, Carter, who defines the power of this approach. He came from a difficult background with a threatening father who had been in prison. Carter echoed his tough demeanour and swaggered around school with his crew. One afternoon, Nadia found him in the stairwell, kicking the wall and sobbing.

'I took him into an empty classroom and asked him what was wrong, but he refused to speak, so I gave him a piece of paper. I told him I was worried he was going to harm himself or someone else so I couldn't let him leave the building, but if he wrote down what he was struggling with I may be able to help. He wrote three words. *I like boys.* And then he said I couldn't ever tell his dad. "He will kill me," he said.'

Nadia's first response was to tell Carter she loved him for who he was and thank him for sharing it with her. Then she said she didn't want him to feel that his life had ended.

'I asked if there was someone at school he liked and he said yes, but he couldn't ever do anything about it. He just knew he was happiest when he was around boys. I told him I got it and I wanted him to know he had a safe space with me, we could discuss anything. Maybe in time it would help him talk to his dad.'

Before his graduation, Carter asked Nadia if he could give a speech on the day. He felt like he had something to say, not just to his own father but to parents in general, about how they need to see their children as individuals. Nadia was thrilled.

'He didn't come out in that speech, but if you knew, then you knew that was exactly what he was doing. He had formed a small group of friends who were either non-conforming or figuring out their identities, so he spoke for them all. It was incredibly powerful. Afterwards he cried and hugged me and his dad came over and said what a great speech it was. As a teacher, your actions could save or change a life.'

I think children can find it easier to talk to a teacher than they do to their own parents – maybe because they are concerned about the reaction, the family expectations that weigh heavy or their fear of upsetting their parents. In some cases, they are worried about bringing shame to the family that can result in being shunned by the community or sent back to their parents' native country. I know this is hard for parents to hear, but how willing are we to be open with our children without making them feel like everything they are doing is wrong? We need to learn to encourage our children to speak by not talking. Our instincts are to get quick answers and step in to solve problems, whereas we need to be patient and create the environment for trust and honesty. For example, those children questioning their identity needed to be given the space to explore how they felt, rather than be shut down, 'talked out of it' or criticised. This is an issue Nadia has come across regularly.

'Parents need to stop making it about them and whether they did something "wrong". This is simply about their child being unique, beautiful, brilliant, exceptional. Parents can't choose what their child wants but they can create a relationship with them where the child feels loved and knows their parents are there for them, unconditionally. That's the only thing that should matter.'

Nadia has witnessed first-hand how situations can escalate and unhappy students become serious threats to themselves, including self-harm and drug abuse. In school, she has worked hard to create an inclusive environment while continuing to uphold school regulations and traditions. It isn't always easy and there have been issues around subjects like toilets (she designated an adult toilet for non-binary use), the colour of graduation gowns (purple was worn by girls, black by boys) and pronouns (it was agreed everyone would be called 'scholars').

'I don't know what it's like to become gender non-conforming and what that means socially and emotionally. I found an organisation that dealt specifically with it and came to school to do professional development with me and my team, as well as running small groups for relevant students. I pushed the boundaries of how far our education system has come in this area. I mean, we use words like diversity and inclusion but how does it really look in our school buildings?'

Every teacher has a personal definition of what this is but, for Nadia, it is to make the child feel they belong. She believes they must be reflected in their environment and have the voice to speak out when that doesn't happen, without being penalised. School is usually their first experience of being in the outside world without their family and it should strengthen their ability to grow and thrive, not strangle it.

'I'm a firm believer in providing children with experiences to prepare them for the world. Without the parameters that stops them exploring what it means to be autonomous. You know, I think we are all, in many ways, representative of our parents and their influence, whether it's positive or negative. We have to be cognisant of that and not repeat mistakes with our own kids, so we must keep the communication open.'

Being present as a parent is crucial and we need to continue to remind ourselves of this because it is easy to let it slip. Nadia learned this with her own daughter, who resented her job when she was younger. Now her daughter is older they have been able to talk more honestly about how she felt.

'I spent so much time being with other children, my own struggled with it. She felt I loved my students more because I was with them longer, bought them things and talked about them a lot. Looking back, she realises how much she had growing up, compared to them. I recognised what she was saying – I wasn't available enough for her. She was present in my space with other kids but I wasn't present with her in the spaces she wanted to be in. So now I make sure I am present in her space. That's the thing I had to learn.'

Francis Jim Tuscano

33, Manila, Philippines

'I want my students to grow up to be resilient people. Of course, I still teach them about studying hard, but if I realise they are not doing well, if they are facing failures, this is not the time to reprimand them. This is the time to show up and tell them it's okay'

Francis Jim Tuscano, who I know as Jim, grew up in Abra, a remote province in the Philippines. The eldest of four children from a Catholic family, he gained a scholarship to study philosophy at university with the idea that he would become a priest or a lawyer. He did neither. Instead, after graduating, he decided to apply for teaching, inspired by his childhood teachers and spurred on by his family circumstances.

'It was more for financial reasons, because I am the eldest and I wanted to help my parents. I have three younger sisters who all needed to be put through college, and I could see how expensive that was. There wasn't time for me to go to law school, and being a priest wouldn't have brought in the money to fund my sisters' studies.'

Jim applied to one of the top Jesuit boys' schools in Metro, Manila, and got the job even though he did not have a formal teaching background. Instead, the combination of his type of degree and studying for a teaching certificate in his first year of employment was enough for him to qualify. He taught Christian life and values education, a religious-based subject required in Catholic schools, and began in Grade 2 with eight- and nine-year-olds.

'Working with younger students taught me about classroom management and not to shout when I needed their attention or when I knew what they were doing was not proper. In the Philippines teachers can be very strict, very traditional. I learned a different approach.'

But it was in his third year of teaching that things really clicked for Jim.

'I got involved with technology, with the use of the iPad, and it reawakened my interest in teaching. Before everything was so repetitive and as a teacher it can be hard not to get bored. It gave me the opportunity to find what would make me stay in this profession. It was technology.'

Jim could see how vital the technological tools were in enabling him to reach students and help them with particular skills and issues, like reading comprehension or sharing what they had learned in class. He has become an advocate of assessing children using non-traditional methods.

'We don't always need to use paper and pen tests. What if we gave children the opportunity to create, you know, videos or audio as artefacts of their learning instead?'

Jim realised the value in empowering students to demonstrate their learning in a way that was comfortable for them.

'I always thought that to be a good teacher, your students have to get good grades. Their high achievement proves you can do, and are doing, your job. Now, I know it is about how you support your students. In the past I have worked with children from varied backgrounds who have different challenges and struggles, and I believe my success is in understanding what they need.'

Jim credits the school with trusting him to find his own way of teaching. He believes being given the opportunity to experiment was the making of him as a teacher. As a department chair now, he is still empowered to look for different ways to lead his colleagues. It is a remarkable, and frustratingly rare, tale of a school recognising a teacher's potential and allowing them to go off on their own tangent.

Jim has raised a hugely important issue about creating the right environment and opportunities to help our young people achieve. For him, the answer is to include technology in everyday learning, and he gives me an example of the impact this has had on one of his students.

'I'm so proud of Gabriel. He's doing an internship right now in the USA. He tells me I influenced him to take computer science.'

Jim taught Gabriel in Grades 2 and 6 and, at the request of his parents, he became his mentor when he went to high school and even, despite the great distance, on to university.

'Gabriel was a high achiever, he would feel bad if he made one mistake. His parents would request a meeting and, in the name of improvement, ask why their son had not got a perfect score. At first, I was really shocked to hear that question simply because it was just a single mistake. I mean, the score is almost perfect, which was still worth celebrating. However, after the meeting, I realised how this kind of mindset, of focusing on getting a perfect score, can deeply affect students – the fear to bring a test paper with one or two mistakes and the pressure to have honours or awards in school, especially since awards in school meant rewards back home.'

Around this time, Jim introduced the iPad as a learning device into the classroom and began experimenting with other forms and strategies for learning, like watching instructional videos, creating infographics and writing their own blogs. He also created new types of assessment, which initially caused stress for his students, including Gabriel, because the tutors they studied with at home did not know how to use technology. This was a brilliant move on Jim's part. He wanted to take students out of their safe study and give them performance-based tests. Some rose to the challenge but it shattered Gabriel's confidence.

'This was my chance to teach Gabriel and his classmates to feel comfortable in making mistakes. And they became more open to feedback. The tests were not a one-shot thing where they made a mistake and got a low grade, they were able to improve on their score the next day and the next.'

I am fascinated by the journey Gabriel took and Jim's attitude to focusing on the person behind the high achiever. One of the tasks Jim set his class was to create their own personal blogs, a record of their reflections that can be shared and discussed with the class.

'There's no right or wrong answer to writing a blog, so it was a challenge for them. I had given them a child-friendly platform but Gabriel didn't like it, he said it was too boring. So, he experimented by creating his own website and okay, that was not the original goal, but it was great.'

This led to Gabriel learning to code in high school and teaching younger students on Saturday mornings – Hackathon Club – before taking a computer science degree. Jim was responsible for unlocking this within him.

'Gabriel told me I gave him the chance to enjoy learning. And the thing about coding, it's about debugging and finding out what is stopping a platform from working, so the first thing you should have is patience and accept that you don't have instant answers. Something Gabriel would have struggled to cope with as a young student.'

Jim is still in touch with Gabriel's parents too. They message him to ask if he will tell their son to slow down and take some rest. It's funny how things change, and Jim acknowledges that he really didn't agree with them when they first met.

'But I think their openness to me and my need to understand what their reasons were resulted in a good relationship. They just wanted the best for their son. We evolved together.'

Continuing to use this approach with students and parents, Jim listens to them, questions their traditional attitude towards perfection and tells them it is okay to make mistakes.

'I say don't put pressure on yourself to be the perfect person, you will miss a lot of things. You will miss the fun of living.'

He recognises these struggles because he was also a high-achieving student and top of his class, graduating with honours, yet he was always scared. He didn't push himself out of his comfort zone or do anything that would affect his grades.

'Now I tell parents this about me so they know that I truly understand and I say, what scares me today is missing the chance of teaching your kids this wisdom about life. I want my students to grow up to be resilient people. Of course, I still teach them about studying hard, but if I realise they are not doing well, if they are facing failures, this is not the time to reprimand them. This is the time to show up and tell them it's okay.'

The students Jim teaches come from privileged backgrounds, unlike him.

'They are the sons of businessmen who own giant companies and airlines. School fees are much higher than a regular school in the country, which is one of the reasons why we have enough funding for technological resources. I have experienced being invalidated as an educator because I teach at an exclusive school but I tell people, I am a product of the public-school system, my mother and sisters teach in the province and that is where my heart is. I never forget where I came from. I do teach in a private school, but it has given me opportunities to also reach out to schools outside my own. I think this is important, I put my own twist on things because I teach values education. I challenge the worldview of these lucky students and tell them they are not the only people in the world. There are others who struggle and it's my job to teach them that too.'

I will be honest, the thought of Jim being invalidated incenses me. Teaching in any school brings challenges and every child has their own issues, regardless of background and social position. What Jim does so brilliantly is show his students the lives beyond the one they live.

Some of them have housekeepers, drivers and chefs. They live in the city. They get driven to and from school in their own cars. In contrast, he tells them, he commutes to school and doesn't have a car, because he lives in a place where it is likely to get stolen. Teaching values education means Jim can expose his students to diverse communities including tribes, indigenous people and the differently abled, and it helps to show them the world outside the comfort of their homes.

'This is the reality. And when I say goodbye to my Grade Six students before they move on to junior high school, my last line to them is to say how proud I will be if they become top businessmen, lawyers, engineers or politicians. But I add that if they forget all the things we have learned, the one thing they must always remember is how to be a good person who thinks of others. And, if I die, and hear they have been unethical, I will get out of my grave and haunt them!'

As well as teaching, Jim is a digital learning consultant, working with organisations and schools to plan a technology programme. But here's the thing: if he is invited to talk about technology, he doesn't talk about technology. Instead he focuses on how we use it to empower students, to give them their own tools to share what they have learned.

I wonder what is the one truth that Jim has discovered about children throughout his career and he answers without hesitating.

'That children come from different contexts and will have different needs. You always start with their context. It's a cliché, but each student is unique and my job is to meet them from where they are coming from.'

As teachers, we know that each of the children in our care have their own story and it is up to us to discover them.

Marjorie Brown

63, Johannesburg, South Africa

'True joy and fulfilment is not just achieving individually but becoming part of the bigger picture that transforms society as a whole'

Marjorie Brown is a white South African teacher, human rights activist, founder of a national children's literature programme and one of my heroines. She is an amazing example of what it takes to teach children to be global citizens. Not that it was ever her intention to do so. Marjorie didn't plan to be a teacher. At school, she preferred science and liked the idea of a career in medicine, but she came from a low-income family and there were no scholarships for university. The only state-sponsored grants available in South Africa were for students who wanted to go into teaching.

'I had thought I would never get to university, even though I had a really good set of marks, because my parents couldn't afford the private fees. Instead I went for a job, but the guy interviewing me looked at my grades and said I shouldn't be asking for a job at this point in my life, I should be at university.'

Marjorie applied for a state teaching bursary and went to Cape Town University. Her teaching subjects were science, maths, history and English. She fell in love with history and this is what she primarily teaches now.

Marjorie's early career path as a teacher was shaped by her cousin, Linelle Gibson, who taught at a school in Cape Town where there were protests against apartheid. Linelle sympathised with the children of colour, and as a result the government blacklisted her and she had to leave the country. Marjorie was deeply affected by this, and knew there was no way she was going to teach at an all-white school to perpetuate the segregation of apartheid. Although she came from a poor background, she knew how lucky she was growing up in a white community, and she couldn't accept the inequality.

'I just don't believe I would have been able to live a decent life knowing what I knew and not doing something about it. Many white South Africans didn't want to know and then they wouldn't have to deal with it. I wanted to be part of a solution and live in an equal society.'

There was a Catholic priest who had left the priesthood and was trying to set up the first non-segregated school in South Africa. He came to speak at Marjorie's university and it was an epiphany for her. Finally, someone was talking about an education system she wanted to be involved in. She approached the priest and told him that she would be keen to be part of his project.

At this time, in the late 1970s, the South African government were trying to keep different groups separate, creating 'homelands', which Marjorie describes as 'dumping grounds on the basis of ethnicity'. Starting a non-segregated school against this backdrop sounds almost impossible. There were seven people involved in the project, including Marjorie, and they raised funds through private business.

'South Africa was in chaos, Soweto, Cape Town . . . Kids took to the streets protesting against the education system and having to learn Afrikaans. As a result of this, big companies realised that reform was needed, so the liberal white businesses gave us money.'

While funds were being raised to build the school, Marjorie and the other teachers sat on the rocks in the scrub and taught their pupils outside.

'We built the school slowly, as we got the money. And that school went on to have a one hundred per cent matric pass rate. From the start my teaching had an element of social justice; it was not just about getting kids out into the workplace but much more about transforming society. There were kids of colour who, for the first time, were getting quality education. It went against the government policy of giving inferior education to people of colour, what they called a "Bantu" education, which groomed them for a life of manual labour.'

Marjorie shares a story with me about one of her most extraordinary students, Moss Mashishi.

'Moss's mother was a domestic worker in Soweto, over three hours away, and she approached me and said, "Look there's no education happening here, please take my child, be his mother, be his teacher."'

It was not uncommon for children to be left on the school doorstep, as the place was considered a haven and the only opportunity for a decent education. For Moss, his mother valued education so much she was willing to sacrifice their life together.

'We found him a family to live with nearby and I would take him away on holidays. He saw the sea for the first time. His mother was living in really difficult circumstances in Soweto. When I became an anti-apartheid activist a few years later I got a flat above an Anglican church and she lived there. It could have put us both in jail but I think what saved us was that people assumed she was the domestic worker. We had to find ways around the laws so that people could retain their dignity.'

And what about Moss?

'He went on to do law at the university in Johannesburg and is now a successful businessman. He was one of the first Black people on the South African Olympic Committee.'

I can tell how proud Marjorie is of him but also how important he was as a catalyst for the next period of her life.

For Marjorie, being a teacher went far beyond the job. It was one of the reasons why she taught history to her students – she wanted to help them understand their past and what was happening in their country. The non-segregated school she and her colleagues built was down the road from the resettlement camps where people had been dumped, which had tin toilets and nothing else.

'I felt I should leave teaching for a while at this point and fight this forced removal of people that was happening around the country. I wanted to play a bigger role in ending apartheid because, even though we were doing a wonderful job with one school, we needed to transform the whole political situation in South Africa so that all kids of colour could have a better education.'

Marjorie joined the Black Sash, a women's human rights group, who raised money and ran advice offices for those who couldn't afford lawyers.

'We had a lot of people coming to us saying they were losing their land to the government and could we help. I became one of three field workers who worked with Black communities in rural areas, helping them to resist forced removals, working with the press, embassies and lawyers to try and stop the process.'

Three years of fighting later and they got a reprieve for all the communities they were working with. This also marked the beginning of the end of apartheid, although it would take several more years to finally stop. During this time, Marjorie sat on national and global policy committees with economists and politicians, working on policy beyond apartheid.

Apartheid finally ended in 1994.

'I thought, "I have done what I set out to do. I have helped fight apartheid. I have helped build new policies. Now I can go back into teaching."'

I am in awe of Marjorie, of her courage, tenacity, compassion and energy. She made a difference in every role and task she undertook, and I want to know: what gave her the strength to keep going?

'People. Just extraordinary people who have an overwhelming sense of social justice and morality. It is like that quote "the only thing necessary for the triumph of evil is for good people to do nothing". Well these people did something. And I was so privileged to work with the finest South Africans who stood for human rights, like Archbishop Desmond Tutu.'

Many of the people Marjorie worked with paid a high price, often facing detention without trial – including her – but, as she points out, they did not experience the level of oppression that people of colour were subjected to when they were detained.

Of all the resources some schools struggle to get hold of, a lack of books is one of the most crucial. Most schools in South Africa don't have school libraries. It won't surprise you to hear that Marjorie did something about that too.

'It's why I started the literary quiz about fifteen years ago with the aim of raising literacy levels across the country. I get books into around a hundred and fifty schools in South Africa that don't have libraries and they are aimed at primary-school-aged children across all reading levels. There is a designated reading champion (usually a teacher) in the school and we organise quizzes around each of the books. I've really seen these schools develop a culture of reading.'

There are countless stories of the children who have benefited from this initiative, but one of Marjorie's favourites is the autistic student who sought refuge in the library. He did not play sport, yet through the quiz he won trophies and was able to travel the world and become recognised by his peers.

Her vision is that every school will have the budget to create a library, but she is enthused by the reading clubs that are multiplying and the discussion about the government embedding the literary quiz within the curriculum.

'I want it to take on a life of its own.'

This urge to change society for the greater good is at the heart of everything Marjorie does. We joke about her desire to achieve world peace, but she would if she could.

'I think my wish would be for everyone to have a greater sense of humility and to truly listen to each other. There is so much division in the world – cultural, racial, sexual, class, gender – we need to take more time to listen and overcome. We have a transformation committee at school, which discusses all these issues and how to make the world more equal. Power is a problem, and being fed large doses of fear and propaganda.'

Marjorie taught in the UK for a while and was aware of how colonialism is absent from the syllabus despite how much it impacted the world. She believes there would be a greater sense of understanding in society if these things were taught at school.

'We're not just educating kids for careers, we want to teach them how to make the world a better place. When I teach children – of course they matter as individuals, but I also want them to be global citizens. And I want them to transcend their own needs and their own wants and desires.'

There is a danger in a competitive school environment for children to become self-seeking, so Marjorie sees it as crucial to instil within them a sense of giving back to the community.

'True joy and fulfilment is not just achieving individually but becoming part of the bigger picture that transforms society as a whole. These are conversations I have with parents too.'

Marjorie also ran the Model United Nations debating at school and her students got involved in leagues attached to local universities and international schools.

'Three of my students helped draft the climate action policy for the city of Johannesburg and one of them, Almaaz Mudaly, spoke at COP26. She's Grade Nine, fourteen years old. How amazing is that? That's the vision I want for all my pupils and I see the parents get excited about seeing the potential in their children, which stretches way beyond the classroom when you give them opportunities.'

Marjorie runs an inner-city social responsibility project that her students support by giving extra numeracy and literacy lessons for orphans within poorer inner-city communities. When COVID happened, her students realised that the children they helped were not able to go to school, which meant they were not being fed.

'For a lot of these kids, their only meal of the day is through the school feeding scheme. My Grade Elevens said that we must create an alternative feeding scheme and so they raised money and food and got those kids fed.'

The same students achieved excellent results and the school had the highest overall average in South Africa. So, despite these students giving their time to others through tutoring and feeding them, they overcame the pandemic with positivity, and their studies were not affected.

This leads us directly to the one truth Marjorie has learned from her students.

'They are greater than we expect them to be. The children I teach are phenomenal. Give them a chance to think beyond themselves and they do. They are inherently empathetic. You know, we tend to think of teenagers as selfish and banal and yet watching my students recently has been a bit like the resurgence of social movements in the 1960s. They have taken up social issues in quite an adult way, whether it's climate change, racism or urban poverty, and they have really risen to the occasion.'

Lucky children, to have Marjorie on their side; and lucky me, for being able to call her a friend.

Mark Reid

41, Vancouver, Canada

'I think we need to stop asking kids what they want to be when they grow up and focus on who they want to be. It's not about finding their identity through the job they do but to recognise the importance of connections and relationships'

Music was everywhere when Mark was growing up in Ontario, Canada. He was part of a band at school and his father was a music teacher. When he was twelve, he decided to become a music teacher himself, following in his dad's footsteps.

At the tender age of fourteen, he chose to leave the small town where he was living with his mum and move to the city to live with his dad, to attend a performing arts high school.

'Looking back, that was a bigger decision than I realised at the time – changing schools, choosing which parent to live with – but it wasn't led by emotion, it was a good kind of selfish.'

Mark wasn't thinking about appeasing his parents, or his teachers, he was thinking about what was right for him. And everyone around him supported him.

'Imagine having an idea at a young age and then every adult you are interacting with throughout your school career is helping to galvanise and support that decision? I mean, it might make me look a little bit stubborn if it weren't for all these external factors that were fuelling this desire.'

Mark became a music teacher at a secondary school, and now he is a hugely respected career resource educator in Vancouver. He teaches in a college-level transition programme supporting teenage students pursuing a career in the skilled trades and technology. I met him several years ago in a hotel bar at a Global Teacher event in Dubai, where he put me at ease immediately. His hospitable spirit and genuine warmth have made him an unofficial ambassador for the Global Teacher Prize family.

Along with his colleague Allison, Mark works with Grade 12 students who don't fit mainstream education for whatever reason, preparing them for apprenticeships or foundation training and placing them in employment. For some students, graduation had been an impossibility until they connected with Mark and Allison and finally found something they were interested in. Mark has always been very aware of the need to champion alternative routes to graduation.

'When I taught band, there were several kids in class who were more interested in the mechanics of the instrument than how they would play it. It was no surprise when they dropped music to take up metalwork or auto mechanics.'

He often meets students who have fallen foul of the system, and he is their last hope. They continually impress him with their resilience, even when they have been ignored or shuffled along, they are still open to those who give time and lift them up.

'I ask students to call me Mark, not Mr Reid, because this period in life is about their transition into adulthood and the workforce. I want to start cultivating skills and attitudes for their next step. It's amazing how much they respond to that. It's about us all as humans – our interactions – not the curriculum.'

In turn the students embrace the opportunities, whether it is in skilled work or, for example, healthcare.

'The kids have realised the world is a mess right now and healthcare is a place where they can go and be productive and helpful. That's a common quality about the students I work with: no matter what type of programme they are pursuing, they want to make a difference.'

Identifying and cultivating a student's strength of spirit is a wonderful thing to witness. When Mark was still teaching music he had a student, Simon, who played the tuba throughout high school.

'He was a solid human, a nice guy and everyone's buddy. He was also physically big; it was just who he was and his body was part of his identity. When the media were interested in me being linked to the Global Teacher Prize, they came to the school and one of the reporters interviewed Simon. And he said, "Mr Reid has made me the best tuba player in the world." Now Simon was not the best tuba player in the world, he just got a little carried away in the moment! Fast-forward to now, seven years later. Simon and I keep in touch and I went with some of his old bandmates to see him compete in a bodybuilding competition. For a kid who was maybe 275 pounds in high school? He's almost half of that now and all muscle and he wasn't just competing, he was winning.'

Mark says Simon is still the same person inside but he has taken the discipline, routine and self-awareness that he gained as a music student to achieve what his adult self wanted. Simon is one of a group of ten boys who were all in Mark's band together and have formed a strong bond with their beloved teacher.

'They are a statistical anomaly. Ten guys who didn't do drugs, alcohol, no teen pregnancies or criminal activity. They have turned into confident adults, all doing totally different things – like finance, healthcare, education, real estate. One is moving to New York to continue working for Apple, but they have stayed closely connected. They each bring something unique to the group and are each other's champions and cheerleaders.'

I wonder what the secret to this is? Mark believes it is the experience of being in a band together.

'And almost all of them were in the volleyball team too on top of being section leaders for the band. They took on what it means to be a team and it stayed with them.'

When Mark bought a house a couple of years ago it was a landmark moment in his life, made even more special by the offer of help from the group, with six of them turning up to paint and install lighting.

'One of them said to me, "We're gonna show up for you because you showed up for us."'

It makes me think of a family, both between the ten students and the ongoing connection they have with Mark.

'Two of the boys lost parents while they were at high school and the group supported them through it. They have transcended the bonds of friendship to become their own type of family too.'

Mark knows he is lucky to have watched this happen and be part of this 'chosen family'.

I know from experience that for as many uplifting stories as the one Mark has just told, there are those students who don't follow the path you hoped they would. Like Mark's fantastic Grade 9 flute player, Oscar, a perceptive, thoughtful student, free from ego.

'Oscar was gifted on his instrument, just brilliant, he had an amazing tone and technique. Any kind of instruction I gave him he got right straight away. And at the end of the year it was almost heartbreaking to find out that he didn't want to continue in band. I sought him out and I told him he was the best fourteen-year-old flute player I had ever taught and he could have a musical future ahead of him. I told him he made it look effortless and I wished I had half as much natural ability. And you know what he said? He said, I know and I don't care, I'm not moved by it.'

I can see how frustrating this must have been for Mark, but he had no choice but to let Oscar go. Every so often during his remaining high school years Mark would check in with Oscar and tell him there was always a place in band for him if he wanted to come back. He never did.

'I was worried that Oscar may never find that thing he could be passionate about. Now he is an adult and manages a barber shop downtown. I like to support former students, so I went to have my hair cut there. There was an important moment for me when I said to him, "You know you could have been an amazing flute player but you didn't want to and it's fine, I'm over it. And I hope you are loving your profession." He stopped what he was doing and he spoke with such passion about his job, about how he was about to open his own barber shop, and that was all I needed to hear.' Oscar did follow through, and opened his shop in the neighbourhood where he grew up.

It's fascinating when we talk about the 'one that got away' and to realise that these students can find their own path somehow. What we hope and expect for them is not always right. Mark's view has changed from persuading a student to give more time to something they may not feel happy with, to supporting their decision.

'I now think, it's okay, if it matters to them they will act on it, and if it doesn't they won't. It is their choice and they will figure it out and if they don't, I am here.'

Exactly this, we are here.

So much of what a teacher does is to find and inspire the passion for a subject in their students, but Mark is evangelical about how we approach this, especially since his conversation with Oscar.

'The thing that I tell young teachers is that we have been telling kids for so long to find their passion and then follow it. And I now just can't help but think this is the worst possible advice to have ever given anyone. Instead we should be saying, find your passion, lead it, monetise it. Once you have found your place and are living an economically sustainable life doing what you love, don't follow it! Lead it.'

I am so impressed by the way Mark looks at things from a different angle and emboldens his students in the process. What would he say to parents whose children are struggling academically or don't fit into the education system?

'I think we need to stop asking kids what they want to be when they grow up and focus on *who* they want to be. It's not about finding their identity through the job they do but to recognise the importance of connections and relationships. We need to show them acknowledgement and support as they find their way. The priority is often the curriculum but if it's at the cost of the humanity in our children, then forget it.'

Maarit Rossi

69, Turku, Finland

'I tell parents you are the role model and the research says that if you are negative about [for example] maths it has a huge impact on your child. They will give up trying. Instead be interested in their maths work and, if they are stuck, involve a family member or friend to help them. Then ask them to show you how they solved it. You can turn the situation around for a positive outcome'

Maarit has a passion for maths. In a teaching career spanning forty years, her mission is to make maths accessible for everyone. As well as working with young students, she trains educators in their approach to the subject and continues to research innovative ways to tackle numeracy learning.

'I am committed to making maths more interesting, even after all these years. You can open a textbook and the content can seem so boring if you don't understand it. Of course, we still need these books, but I have found other ways to learn. I think this has been the second most important thing about my career. The first is the students I have taught.'

As a young teacher in Finland, Maarit was disappointed by the curriculum, the structure of the lessons and the methods of teaching. During a work trip to the UK with colleagues, they were faced with a problem-solving task that individually defeated them; but together, they succeeded. This was the catalyst for Maarit and she took her discovery back to her own classroom.

'Students are active learners. We need to change the classroom from teacher-centred to student-centred and understand that some learning benefits from being done more organically, like in a group, or outside or with a practical reason. It's more about being a mentor than a teacher. We should be guiding, not leading. In maths, students must understand the basic theory but then they can be empowered to put it into practice, and working in a group is key. My students often come to me after a lesson to ask what we will be doing in the next one. They can't wait! These are my best moments.'

Maarit believes everyone can learn maths but that there is a misconception that you are either good or bad at the subject, and this can isolate students who think they are weak at it. She sees parents reinforce this by saying, 'Oh, I wasn't very good at maths' so the child assumes they won't be either. I know I have been guilty of this with my own children, so how do we avoid falling into this trap?

'I tell parents you are the role model and the research says that if you are negative about maths it has a huge impact on your child. They will give up trying. Instead be interested in their maths work and, if they are stuck, involve a family member or friend to help them. Then ask them to show you how they solved it. You can turn the situation around for a positive outcome.'

Another way to successfully tackle this subject in the classroom is to put maths into a practical environment where students see the point of their numeracy skills. Twenty-five years ago, Maarit developed a school project with the help of the Red Cross. It was based on data from a refugee camp in Africa and the students had to work out what and how much food they needed for the one million plus people as well as the cost, the number of times the packages should be delivered and how many drivers this took. This taught the students lessons on many levels, not just in maths. Maarit encourages parents to take a similar tack at home, setting their children tasks like working out how much water the household uses in a week or measuring out ingredients for baking.

Maarit's focus is not just on maths and science but on cultural experiences and she has organised foreign trips for her students, including a memorable jaunt to Hungary. On this occasion, she took the class who had been under her care for several years, so she was close to them all. Maarit's students were so appreciative of their trip to Hungary they put together a scrapbook of their week including all the wonderful things they had learned and memories they had made, and presented it to her.

'It was such a reward for me. They were a special group. They learned ten times more in one week than they would have learned at school. One girl stood out for her work ethic. She was from a single-parent family and very talented but she didn't believe in herself. I think she also made an impression because my mother was a single parent at one point so I know how hard it can be for everyone. I know this student is now a single mother and very successful in her job.'

For all the children who have thrived in Maarit's care, there is one she remembers wistfully. Tina was a difficult student who was fighting personal demons. Despite being clever, she did not do very well at school and after she left, Maarit heard that she had begun taking drugs. Maarit has seen Tina twice in the years following. The first time was when Tina and a group of friends, all in their early twenties, returned to the school with the idea of causing trouble at an event that celebrated students. One of the teachers came to find Maarit, unsure of what to do as they were refusing to leave.

'I went up to the group and immediately recognised Tina, but I didn't say anything. They were all dirty, smelled terrible and I thought they had been taking drugs. I shook each of them by the hand, which surprised them, and then I explained that the event was by invitation only and I would appreciate it if they left. And they did, calmly.'

Three years later Maarit met Tina again. This time she was a cleaner in Maarit's school, the same one she had been a student at.

'I was so happy to see her. We talked for a long time. Tina's problem had always been her identity. She was a girl but she felt she should be a boy, so she was very confused. I don't know how she survived the turbulence because she didn't discuss it but, when we spoke, I knew she had found balance in her life.'

Maarit has learned many lessons from over forty years of teaching.

'I love to work with children because they are so honest. And if there is a problem or a disagreement it gets solved quickly and they move on. This does not happen with adults. In fact, I once dealt with two girls who had been fighting and then their mothers came into my office. They began to fight. I told them I would not stand for it and sent them all out.'

Generally speaking though, Maarit has enjoyed being involved with her pupils' parents throughout her long-standing career. She has worked in four different schools, and became principal at her last school, Kirkkonummi, a municipality half an hour from Helsinki. There were six hundred students in her care and around fifty teachers. She believes part of the school's good reputation was down to the parents who supported the staff and championed the education.

'Parents wanted to know how they could help their children at home and I said it's really simple. Just ask them how their day was. Ask them what they learned, was it difficult and what they would like to share about it. They are very easy questions. Sometimes parents think they should be studying with their children but no, the students should take responsibility for their own studies. Parents just need to be interested and change their questions slightly each day to avoid automatic responses. And listen to the answers they give because otherwise students begin to think the work they are doing is not so important. We must listen well.'

Ranjitsinh Disale

34, Barshi, India

'Ultimately education means to bring change in society. And if I see that something wrong is happening, it's my duty, my responsibility, to try and stop it'

Ranjit has never forgotten what one of his students said to him. Rahul was nine years old and a pupil at the tiny village school in Paritewadi, in the Solapur district of Maharashtra. Like many of Ranjit's students, Rahul came from a deeply religious farming family and, although a quiet, thoughtful child, he made a big impact on his teacher. Every day the class would lunch together, sharing their tiffin boxes of curries and rice, and it was during one of these breaks that Rahul spoke about his faith.

'He was talking about his belief in the principles of sharing, how when God gives you something it's meant to be shared and this action will bring you closer to God. I call it the Philosophy of Rahul and I now believe in it too, the experience of sharing, whatever it may be.'

Every day Ranjit shares his knowledge with his students and in return, he says, he is rewarded with their happiness, the satisfaction of their parents and a community of people who believe in him. It's a powerful transaction. And as for Rahul, he is now eighteen and is practising what he preached as a little boy, maintaining his connection with his farming background by studying business administration in agriculture, with a vision to progress and modernise the sector. Ranjit is incredibly proud of him and they continue to share a mutually inspirational relationship.

Ranjit never imagined being a teacher when he was younger. His dream was to become an engineer. He enrolled in engineering college when he was eighteen, but it proved too difficult an environment for him and he had to leave after one semester.

'I was bullied by the other students. I was very shy, I never came out of my house and I didn't know how to interact with people, I was not expressive at the time. They bullied me and so I left.'

Back at home Ranjit's father was worried about his career and future, so he enrolled him into the nearest teacher training college. It wouldn't have been Ranjit's first choice. His father was a teacher and Ranjit knew how hard the job was and the difficulties teachers faced in India, including being expected to build their classrooms, acquire the school equipment needed and provide midday meals for students. Less of a schoolteacher and more of a business owner, wading through administrative work, community liaison, and practical and welfare issues.

Ranjit told his father he was very hesitant, and they struck a deal. Ranjit would give it six months and, if he didn't enjoy it, then he could join a new engineering college and still have the chance to pursue his dreams. Yet, those six months at the teacher training college were a revelation to him. He saw the difference a great teacher could make to a student's life, the importance of the role and the impact he could have. There was a pivotal moment in the process. One morning, still early in the course, the teacher asked students to prepare a five-minute lesson plan and then present it to the others in the class. He was one of the first to be called up.

'I had prepared my piece but I couldn't speak. I just said a couple of lines and then my brain stopped working. I couldn't continue. I had lost complete confidence in myself and I remember looking at my teacher, with tears in my eyes, desperately hoping he would let me off the hook and tell me to sit back down.'

Instead, his teacher asked everyone to start clapping and chant his name: 'Ranjit! Ranjit! Ranjit!' The swell of vocal and visible support triggered something in Ranjit's brain. He stopped crying and made his presentation. Later, he went to find his teacher in the staffroom, hugged him and cried again, this time with tears of joy. His teacher said his job was to give students confidence. He had seen something in Ranjit that shone out, so he had grabbed hold of it, and was determined to make his student a teacher. This was a small yet significant moment, which not only changed Ranjit's life but enabled him to do the same for others. It was like a rebirth into teaching.

When Ranjit first started, he set up his classroom in an old cattle shed that was still being used to house some cows. He had nothing – no desks, chairs, equipment or electricity. The owner of the shed, a powerful local politician, had voluntarily given it to the government for the purpose of turning it into a classroom. Ranjit knew he could transform it with the help of the community, so he asked for financial and practical help – spare chairs, a hand with the painting, cash donations. He knew he could create a pleasant space. While learning can thrive on very little, there is something incredibly important about the environment a teacher creates. Students benefit hugely from an ordered, calm learning space surrounded by displays of work – it is when the magic happens. This is exactly what Ranjit did with the derelict cowshed.

Then the politician decided he wanted it back. He saw the space was clean and functional and he wasn't comfortable with a teacher and children coming from another village. Ranjit was devastated.

'At first, I asked him if I could please just be allowed to keep it, but he was very hesitant and abusive and I backed off. I did not want to match anger with anger. Then one day I arrived on a motorbike, which I had borrowed from a friend of mine as the journey from my village was long, and the politician came up with his children and they broke the bike. And I was telling them, my God, no, this is not my bike, it's my friend's bike and I am not in a position to pay for it.'

I can't imagine how awful that moment was for Ranjit – he cites it as the lowest point in his teaching career – or how it would feel to fight so hard for a space for children to learn in. How could the politician, a respected member of his community with children of his own, change his mind about a lowly shed that could be life-changing for young people? Other teachers didn't understand Ranjit's objections and told him not to fuss, the teaching could still happen outside in the field; but he did not agree.

'India was talking about being a superpower country. How can we be such a thing when we look at how we are treating the citizens of the future? I struggled a lot in the beginning, particularly with other people's mindsets. And I thought, no, I will teach my students in a classroom and I want to give them the best possible experience.'

Ranjit managed to reclaim the space in 2009 when the politician stepped back.

Ranjit has gone from teaching seven- to nine-year-olds in a classroom he shared with cattle, to a designated learning space with technology. What hasn't changed over this time is his attitude and approach to his students, and he has never forgotten what his college teacher taught him about inspiring confidence.

'I like to connect with them more emotionally, to understand their backgrounds, family and behaviour outside my classroom.'

Teaching in a village means a level of respect from the community, but also a familiarity, and the villagers' doors are always open to him. This relationship doesn't stop once the student leaves the school – Ranjit continues to counsel and support past pupils and their families.

'And it is most important, I think, because we know that education is looked at as a problem-solver. So problems are everywhere, but only education brings solutions. It's not enough to just teach them, it's also about building relationships that will last past childhood, through teenage years and beyond. So, what I do in my classrooms every day is to share life lessons and stories that will encourage them to do great things.'

Rahul is a great example. Ranjit had spotted a potential in him that he wanted to help fulfil, just as Ranjit's teacher had done with him during his training. He took Rahul and another student, Shruti, to a government-initiated drama project, which meant they would need to take the train. Neither Rahul nor Shruti had ever been on a train before, and they were full of excitement for the three-hour journey and what lay beyond. I can see how hard Ranjit works to open as many doors as possible for his students and that he wants them to be the very best they can be, for themselves, not for their family, village or country. It echoes my own approach to and experience of teaching. Some of the children in my school have not been on a bus or a train, although the underground is right next to the school building. Their local community is their home and they do not venture beyond it. It is our job to show them there is a bigger world out there and to enable them to go out into it when they are ready.

Similarly, one Saturday afternoon, Ranjit was invited to a wedding by a colleague and because, like me, he is never one to turn down the opportunity for food and dancing, he said yes. When he and his colleague arrived, they realised the bride was an ex-student of Ranjit's, Priya, brilliant at maths and just fourteen years old. Although underage marriages were still common at the time, they were illegal, so Ranjit's colleague called the police, who rushed over, stopped the wedding and took everyone into custody.

'Somebody told the bride's family it was me who called the police and they all barged into the room in the house I was staying in. It was a very tense situation. I did have to call the police a couple of days later to seek protection.'

The police met with community members to defuse the situation and invited Ranjit to join them, telling the group they were authorising him to report any underage illegal marriages. It wasn't Ranjit's job to do so, but the police saw the power in him as a teacher and as an individual.

'Ultimately education means to bring change in society. And if I see that something wrong is happening, it's my duty, my responsibility, to try and stop it.'

And what happened to Priya? Ranjit learned that her mother had pushed for an early marriage because the family was poor and they had found her a rich husband. They were also keen to protect her from unwanted mental and sexual harassment (which starts from a young age), so thought she would be safe if she became her husband's responsibility. Her marriage cancelled, Priya returned to school to finish her education, feeling relieved, but worried about her future. A little while later her fiancé met up with Ranjit.

'I was worried he would abuse me, but he told me that I had stopped them committing a crime that could have seen him spend eight years in prison. I didn't expect him to be so mature. He thanked me. They did marry when Priya turned eighteen, and she is now doing a Master's in engineering.'

Everything Ranjit does, he does with passion, and he encourages his students to do the same and for their parents to support them in this approach.

'I tell them, whatever you do, do your best. Whether it's a big thing or little, it doesn't matter, put your heart into it. There can be amazing returns and big changes made from a life lived that way.'

I think Ranjit's superpower is the ability to give others confidence at exactly the point they need it, just as he was given it many years ago.

Andrew Moffat

50, Birmingham, UK

'Within my classroom I see children debating
issues, questioning beliefs and holding me
to account daily and it shows their growing
confidence, passion and how much they care.
This makes me think I am succeeding'

Andrew Moffat is a fabulous force of nature. We first met a few years ago, when he sat next to me on the back row of a bus that was taking a group of teachers to a conference. It was comradeship at first sight. A UK primary school teacher in Birmingham for over twenty-five years, Andrew was in 2017 awarded a deserved MBE for his services to equality in education. He is also no stranger to controversy, following several high-profile incidents in his teaching career. Talking to him about his experience is both thought-provoking and, at times, shocking, but what shines bright is his commitment to learn from these situations, the care and respect he shows for his students and his love of the teaching profession.

Growing up in the 1970s and 80s, Andrew was systematically bullied at school for being gay, although he didn't come out until he was an adult. This early experience shaped the person and the teacher he became and he was determined to help other children who were struggling. He created a teaching resource – *Challenging Homophobia in Primary Schools* – and taught lessons on tolerance, causing several parents (some from the Christian and Muslim communities) to complain, stating that Andrew was guilty of homosexual indoctrination. Andrew says he made two mistakes.

'It had gone wrong for two reasons. Number one, I had focused on a single issue and so therefore it was seen as "gay lessons", which it wasn't, but it's hard to argue when the word "homophobia" is in the title of the resource. Secondly, I never engaged the parents. I was naïve, I thought why make a fuss about it? But of course, not everyone's on the same page and you've got to bring the people with you.'

Andrew resigned from the school and vowed to learn from his community next time and build a bridge to a better understanding. He applied for an assistant headteacher post at a different Birmingham school, but was clear about his intentions from the beginning.

'I explained what had happened in my last job and that I would be great in this new role but I still had much work to do in the area of equality. I said, please do not employ me if in a year, you are going to say we can't do this. I only want you to employ me if you are going to support me to do this.'

He got the job and the support. There was an inflammatory national press piece around him resigning from his previous job, which prompted a flurry of media interest, but he steered through it admirably. It happened the week before he was due to start his new job, so he went to see the headteacher to apologise, concerned that she may have got cold feet, but 'she gave me a big hug, asked if I was okay and then said she would see me on Monday. That's what you want, isn't it?!'

Emboldened by the challenges he had overcome and for those still ahead, Andrew founded an initiative that took its title, No Outsiders, from one of Archbishop Desmond Tutu's speeches about inequality: 'Everyone is an insider, there are no outsiders, whatever their beliefs, whatever their colour, gender or sexuality.' This deeply resonated with

Andrew and he developed a programme, using the Equality Act as the foundation, teaching children at school that everyone is welcome.

'There's no hierarchy; the Equality Act covers everything from race and religion to LGBTQ and gender. They all count equally. It is about inclusion.'

The programme gained traction quickly, resulting in the Home Office employing him to go to Newcastle to combat concerns about the English Defence League in thirteen schools there. The word spread and other schools adopted No Outsiders, with Andrew working on it one day a week.

'I could have gone freelance and worked on the project full-time but I didn't want to stop teaching. I wanted to stay at school, and keep the credibility of being a teacher and continue to learn from those challenges.'

It was on Christmas Eve 2018 that the story took a difficult turn. The government released long-overdue updated guidance for primary schools on dealing with sex education.

'There was nothing really new in there apart from a couple of paragraphs about same-sex families; it was all a bit woolly. The responsibility to tackle this was more on the shoulders of secondary rather than primary schools, which were told they only need cover it when they considered it appropriate to do so. That was it.'

In response to the government guidance a YouTube video, filmed at the Islamic Unity Conference, began to circulate claiming the change to the curriculum was 'a war on morality and on our spirituality . . . the core of it is an assault on families.'

'It was incredibly incendiary and I watched it and my blood ran cold. It was the Christmas holiday, so there was no opportunity to address this with parents until the new year. By which time it had escalated.'

One of my most sincere teacherly wishes is for parents to trust us and let us do our job – I think concerns often come from a place of fear. Andrew was worried his work through No Outsiders would be hijacked by the furore from the conference. On the first day back at school he spoke to parents and was reassured that there were no issues. The day after came the first protest. What began with three mums standing outside the school gate with a petition saying, 'Stop sexualising our children' developed quickly.

'In the space of a week we had three hundred parents protesting outside the school from 8.30 a.m. for an hour. They were chanting, "Get Mr Moffat out!" Any approach I made to speak to them was filmed for social media. There were all sorts of ridiculous accusations made against me that weren't true. It was awful. The problem was they didn't really want to listen to me.'

Andrew had become a scapegoat for the issue. I cannot imagine how he coped throughout this time, but luckily his school whole-heartedly supported him. The worst part for him was seeing his students standing outside protesting with their parents.

'In one sense it was very exciting for the children, shouting, "Get Mr Moffat out!" with their parents, but then they had to come in to school and be taught by me. It was a confusing and traumatic situation for them to be in.'

Andrew recounts an assembly he led when he began by saying, 'Good morning everyone!' and there was complete silence.

'The children did not feel able to say, "Good morning" back to me.

I tried again and a few looked around at the others but still nobody responded. It was agony and I debated whether it was appropriate to make them say it and I thought, yes, it was so I said, "Come on, you know what you have to do so let's try it once more, because it would be a shame if we had to practise this in your break time" and they begrudgingly did it. It wasn't ideal and I did suggest I stopped doing assemblies after that, but the head insisted I carry on.'

Actions speak louder than words and Andrew soon found anonymous notes of support on his desk from his protesting students.

'The children weren't able to publicly defend me but they wanted me to know they cared. They had their own minds and they knew what was right and wrong, what was mean and kind. It was a revelation and reinforced why I am a teacher.'

As well as this and the fantastic support he received from his teacher colleagues, the word spread to the local community and beyond, resulting in an outpouring of love.

'My school was inundated with cards and gifts from every corner of society including other schools, LGBTQ groups and church groups, all thanking us for the work our school was doing against inequality and hate. My Twitter feed exploded and was full of messages encouraging me to keep going. The protests reminded me of some of the best elements of being in the teaching profession and a member of a bigger community.'

Andrew is brave and resilient – I think he is one of the most amazing educators I have ever met. He has turned No Outsiders into a charity, with a vision to 'prepare young people and adults for life as global citizens, reduce potential for terrorism and promote community cohesion'. It is used by hundreds of schools across the country.

Andrew now splits his time between teaching in the primary school classroom and training colleagues on how to use the programme.

'My first slide is always the latest hate crime statistics. It increases every year, last year by nine per cent. Why isn't there an outcry about this? I don't see anyone with a plan. So I have a plan and it's this: education, education, education. We have to teach children to embrace and enjoy diversity and not be frightened of it. The thought of a child in my class punching someone in ten years' time because they are Black, gay, transgender . . . my aim is to teach children to be kind and feel part of this country.'

I don't want to cast a shadow over this conversation but I want to know if Andrew feels he is succeeding? His response is enthusiastic and reassuring.

'Absolutely. No question at all, because of the number of schools who are doing my work. Not only that but within my classroom I see children debating issues, questioning beliefs and holding me to account daily and it shows their growing confidence, passion and how much they care. This makes me think I am succeeding.'

Andrew has had more than his fair share of difficult times, but he knows some of the children's stories are much harder to bear. One of the earliest pupils who had an impact on him was six-year-old Jane, who was going to be adopted and leave the school. She was so excited and her classmates threw a big leaving party for her. But within a matter of months, the adoption had broken down and Jane was back.

'It was the most awful thing for her to go through and she was broken by it because she really wanted a family. Another placement was found and we were all incredibly nervous about it. But this time the prospective parents came to visit me in the classroom several times and they were lovely. On Jane's last day, her new parents came to collect her and took a photograph of us together. We didn't hear from them again and I hoped beyond hope that everything had worked out for that little girl. Fast-forward many years and I am in the middle of the highly public protests when I get a message from Jane's mum. She had seen me on the news and she wanted me to know that her daughter was now a happy adult with a great job, husband and child. And the photo of the two of us is still stuck on her fridge. Her mother said, she sends you all her love. So that is what teaching is about, isn't it?'

Andrew is used to challenging situations. He ran a behaviour unit for seven years, trying to get children who had been excluded from mainstream education back into it.

'It is associated with the school, so we can reintegrate them before they head to secondary school, although it doesn't always work out that way.'

One boy, Scott, was at a different behaviour unit first. When Andrew went to meet him Scott had scaled the furniture and climbed to the top, touching the ceiling, and was refusing to come down.

'The teacher said to me this is what he does, you won't get him down when he comes to your place. And I thought, well let's see about that. I don't give in easily. Scott was one of our early success stories. He messaged me when he saw the press stuff around the protests and it meant such a lot to me.'

Having confidence is a life skill that Andrew wants us all to access.

'When I was thirteen I used to hide my ABBA records when friends came over because I was terrified of what they would think of me. And as an adult, the protest experience took its toll on my confidence as a teacher. I stepped out of the classroom and focused on No Outsiders for a while, but being away from day-to-day teaching made it harder to move on from what went before. So I returned, and it was absolutely the best thing I could have done. I am most proud of being a class teacher.'

I feel the same. For everything we have achieved so far and the plans we have for the future, I am most fulfilled when I am in the classroom with my students. It is a mix of challenge, therapy and growth. It's also exhausting and keeps me on my toes, but that keeps me young!

'Exactly! You've got to love what you are doing,' Andrew says, 'it's hard work but going in every day, it's where I am meant to be. Actually, I love being Mr Moffat . . .'

I am so glad there are Mr Moffats in our schools.

Maggie MacDonnell

Nova Scotia, Canada

*'It's impossible for me to be the expert
in their reality, but I can be the
expert in dreaming with them'*

Salluit is a fly-in Inuit community located in the Arctic region of Nunavik, Quebec, Canada. Temperatures can reach −60 Celsius with a winter that lasts for more than eight months. Sitting near the Hudson Bay, it is home to a rapidly growing Inuit population of nearly 2,000. The Inuit are an Indigenous group that has been living in these regions for over 15,000 years, but colonial practices have caused major upheaval in the last few generations. The panoramic tundra takes your breath away as do the haunting stories of colonial trauma that so many residents also hold within their hearts. There are reflected in the high rates of unemployment, sexual abuse, gender inequality, poverty and the rising number of youth suicides.

It is there that Nova Scotia-born Maggie MacDonnell took a teaching job after doing a Master's degree at the University of Toronto. Maggie had been working and volunteering in the community development field for several years in East Africa, acquiring new skills and learning about the devastating impact of colonisation. Her university studies led her towards topics of gender, inclusion, race and empowerment. As a white, female Canadian she also wanted to further understand the history of her own country, so much of it rooted in oppression towards Indigenous groups.

'I was working in the community development field in East Africa, but I was thinking the same approaches would be really valuable in Canada too. I thought to myself, maybe I can connect with some of the Indigenous communities there. It is well known that there is a chronic shortage of teacher in these isolated communities, so that represented a way to connect with them.'

She knew the majority of the challenges the Inuit faced were rooted in colonial history and that as a result, the youth were facing a lot of trauma. Historically, Inuit families had been displaced by the government and herded into settlements where the government promised housing, health provision and education. Instead the communities were largely abandoned and promises broken, resulting in countless traumas, and there remains huge anger and distrust towards the government. Not only that, but their children were taken away from them.

It is only in recent years that the full extent of the appalling level of abuse and suppression of the Inuit community has come to light for the larger Canada population, and Maggie is full of quiet rage about it.

'Generation after generation of Indigenous children were ripped from their families and their homes as they reached the age of five or six, and were taken thousands of kilometres away to boarding schools. These schools were usually run by the Catholic Church or another Christian religious organisation, with support from the government.'

The children were not allowed to speak their language and all their cultural references were stripped from them. There are also terrible stories of young girls being impregnated by the priests who ran the school, the same men who would then deliver the babies and dispose of them in the school incinerator. The last school closed in 1996.

The shocking discovery of the mass graves of Inuit children at these schools across Canada hit the national and international news in 2021. Of course, Indigenous survivors of these schools used to tell these stories, but their experiences were often minimised or dismissed. Now there is undeniable physical evidence and, because of what is now publicly known, it is considered to be an act of genocide.

'We call those adults who went through this school system "residential school survivors", because a lot of kids didn't make it. And the survivors shared memories of being asked to dig holes in the fields that surrounded the schools and how regularly their fellow students would just go missing. There were many children who never went home. I think at this point they have found over seven hundred skeletal remains across the country, but they are expecting the tally to rise significantly, most likely thousands and thousands will be found. There is still a lot of racial tension and huge mistrust towards the white settler population. Understandably.'

Not only was Maggie teaching students who carried this intergenerational trauma, but they were still living in a failing system.

'Education is underfunded, the healthcare system is a disaster, there is poor internet and no highways to access the northern Arctic. These people are dealing with awful economic, social and environmental hardships.'

When Maggie first started teaching there, her students were attempting to survive in the face of food insecurity, a crisis of shelter (with kids sofa-surfing) and a huge distrust of the school system.

'Although the schools are now largely run by Inuits, the funding is still largely controlled by the government. There is so much trust-building still to be done, you know, it's unsurprising that there is no strong cultural expectation for children to come to school. In many communities the drop out rate can be as high as ninety per cent.'

The number of young people taking their own lives has been and continues to be at a crisis point. Without doubt the hardest situation Maggie dealt with was the tragic loss of students to suicide. She attended their funerals and the following day found herself standing in the classroom with an empty chair and desk.

'Attending suicide funerals for lost students is haunting, and also creates a sense of urgency. I knew that we – myself and the school – had to somehow pivot to better address the realities of our students. I don't think in terms of how many of my students graduate. Sometimes I am winning just because they're alive. I can remember baking a cake for a student's birthday and she stunned me when she said, you know, I never thought I would make it to sixteen. She had lost so many people to suicide, she assumed it was going to be her ending too.'

Maggie tells me how she learned from some of her more resilient students. She recounts a story about how a pupil, well-loved in the community, took his own life. When she heard the news she immediately thought of all the people close to him who would be affected, maybe enough to do it too.

'It was such a tragic moment. For the boy, his family and his friends. My mind was spinning, doing a sort of social mapping of who they were all connected to and how far-reaching the impact would be.'

The person Maggie was most worried about was the boy's older brother. The other students formed a protective force shield around him, taking it in turns to accompany him wherever he went and handing over at different times. This was not instigated or led by a teacher or a parent, it was something the children emotionally responded to.

'It was like an unofficial schedule and he was never on his own, as he walked from school to the fitness centre, or from the youth house to dinner at his cousin's . . . they knew how vulnerable he was and they were there for him. I will never forget their compassion, their teamwork, their complete understanding of the situation. It's not easy to be with someone in such a deep state of suffering who may want to push you away. They held firm and they were keeping that kid alive, as far as I saw it.'

Maggie believes that teenagers are the real frontline workers in any youth crisis, knowing much more than a social worker, counsellor or nurse and instinctively understanding how to deal with big issues.

'It was about observing and listening. I needed two eyes, two ears and one mouth to keep shut from judgement. I would just watch them a lot and get to know them, and connect however I could, even through social media.'

Maggie was assigned an alternative class of kids who had, or were at risk, of dropping out. She had the most difficult, disruptive, uninterested and disillusioned bunch of eleven- to eighteen-year-olds and she was their last chance at formal education.

'I needed to authentically connect to these kids beyond the historical reasons why they didn't want to connect with me. With their permission, I wanted to reach them and their community and, if they allowed me to go deep enough, then maybe the magic could happen.'

It was incredibly hard to begin with as she tried to find ways to reach out to them, but then she had a small epiphany.

She was lucky to work in a project-based classroom that gave her the freedom to teach in an alternative way, calling her class 'Life Skills'. She wanted to empower her students to become agents of change, and to use education to create better realities for themselves.

'I learned that most of my class were basically a gang of bike thieves and I could see that there was a lot of resentment towards them in the community. I decided to see their behaviour as an asset, a talent, something hopeful. Instead of seeing them as thieves I'll see them as kids who love bikes! Great, let's work with this.'

Maggie set up a bike workshop and found an ally in a bike mechanic who described himself as an anarchist. His demeanour was the exact opposite of a stereotypical teacher who loves order, discipline and routine. She knew he would understand how to communicate with the kids he would be working with and she secured enough funding to pay for him to come up for three weeks.

'It's impossible for me to be the expert in their reality, but I can be the expert in dreaming with them.'

On the first day of the bike class, three students showed up. On the second day, only two; but within a week, all fifteen of Maggie's students were in the class. They began mending and building their own bikes and then started to create bike ramps and trails.

'The community saw that the kids were so happy building their own bikes, they had stopped stealing everyone else's. And then something even more amazing happened – the same people would bring their bikes to the kids to get them fixed. The very same bikes my students used to steal. The way I like to tell it, they weren't just learning how to fix a bike, they were learning how to fix their relationships with the community.'

Finding a pathway to these young people, using something they love, is a great achievement for Maggie, but being able to make it work for the greater good was like 'riding the magic train to happiness', as she puts it.

Maggie also used exercise as a coping tool to help students deal with depression and the chronic stress they were under. She took the bike project a step further by starting a school nutrition programme.

'I found this amazing bicycle that you could attach a blender to so, as you pedalled, it powered the blender. Everyone queued up to make smoothies. You know how much energy a Grade Seven boy has? I would put that energy into a twenty-minute pedal that would make one hundred smoothies and my students would distribute them to the whole school. So instead of other pupils avoiding my "drop-out" students at all costs, they were like "Hey Joey, can I have a raspberry smoothie?" I created helpful leadership roles for my students where they could assist their peers. It changed the whole dynamic. They were no longer the scary bully bike thieves, they were fixing your bike and making you tasty smoothies!'

So too did the sport programmes Maggie set up including a running club that saw her students ditch their cigarettes and which resulted in students running (and winning) marathons around the world.

'I always said to my students that when you run by yourself you go fast, but when you run with others you can go so far. This was a saying from Tanzania. It has such a profound community and collectivist message.'

All the programmes she has built have been about cultivating resilience, hope and self-belief in her students. But I want to know how she gave these young people faith in their future? Not many people would have the stamina and fortitude to work in a school and community like the one Maggie chose. What was it that drove her?

'I'm so lucky to be a Canadian and have all this tremendous privilege, and yet we must recognise we stand on top of a lot of people's shoulders. I hope this doesn't sound like "great white saviour" talk, that's absolutely not who I am or what I believe. It's about being human. I think there's a tremendous responsibility to open our eyes to social injustice. Surely a life worth living is a life worth diving into even when it's messy, ugly and murky and we, and it, are flawed? It is about living an authentic life.'

I can't imagine any student not being captivated and changed by having Maggie in their life. Like the student who went from constantly being in the principal's office and being suspended, to becoming a graduate who works as a teaching assistant in the school. That is just one example of the impact Maggie's teaching has had.

'My students made me a better person. They taught me stuff about myself and the world. You know, people come to the Arctic and are mesmerised by the land but what inspires me is the youth there. I believe they are the true northern lights.'

Well said, Maggie, you profound, fierce, wonderful woman.

Peter Tabichi

40, Nakuru, Kenya

'Never surrender. Keep looking for the best solution on how to give support. Sometimes I have to think of other creative ways to engage them and then I see change'

Peter Tabichi says to be a great teacher you should do more and talk less. As a Franciscan monk, he practises this philosophy in all areas of his life as well as in his role as a science, maths and physics teacher in a small rural Kenyan school. He gives away eighty per cent of his salary to local community initiatives focused on education, sustainability and peace, and is passionate about building a better life for his students. Peter won the esteemed Global Teacher Prize the year after me and I couldn't have handed the baton to a worthier successor. An hour in his company is an invaluable and inspirational treat; he never fails to lift my spirits when we speak.

The son of a teacher father, Peter knew this career path was his destiny. He lost his mother when he was still a child, a difficult age to deal with such a devastating loss, and it felt as if his entire world had fallen apart. It was just one of the challenges he faced as he navigated his way through school – first primary and secondary, followed by college – and he talks of each stage with such surprise that he made it through and on to the next. He cites miracles and the support of his father and his teachers that made it possible.

'I didn't even know if I would finish primary school. I grew up in a very humble background and it was a struggle to get quality education.

For me it was luck. I think if you are in a challenging environment, then positive transformation can come from that. Don't get stuck in it. Otherwise what are you solving?'

Peter teaches in a community similar to the one he grew up in. Sponsored by the government, Keriko Mixed Day Secondary School is in the semi-arid Pwani Village, nestled in a remote part of the Rift Valley in Kenya where they battle drought, famine, poverty and food deprivation. Children from a mix of religions and cultures face many obstacles, including walking vast distances just to get to their classroom every day. The majority of Peter's students are from poor families – nearly a third are orphans – and vulnerable to drug abuse, suicide, underage marriage and teen pregnancy. Peter's optimism is undiminished by the hardship and the total lack of facilities and infrastructure available, either at home or at school. It is a situation he is well used to.

'When I was a child my school was a mud hut and we didn't have enough of anything, no library, or electricity for light, no shoes and not even a hardwood floor. There was so much dust everywhere, all the time, our spit was full of it. Everything we learned came from the teachers standing in front of us, we relied on them.'

Peter has become the teacher he was taught by and then more besides. He has established a series of clubs to benefit different sections of the school and wider community that have each become hugely successful. His science club beat some of the best schools in the country at Kenya's respected Science and Engineering Fair in 2018, winning with their measuring invention to help deaf and blind people. The team then went on to qualify for the international fair in the USA, as well as winning an award for generating electricity from plant life. At the time, Peter said how immensely proud of his students he was, particularly as they had achieved so much with so little and, as a teacher, how important a positive impact was, not just for the country but for Africa. This wider approach is evident in his work outside the classroom teaching the local farming community how to grow crops resistant to famine, and through his peace work against tribal violence, uniting the students of the seven tribes through shared assemblies and encouraging them to take it in turn to lead the worship.

In the time he has been teaching at the school, enrolment has doubled and behaviour dramatically improved, showing, Peter says, that it is about empowering each student to believe they can do it.

'If students can see they are working towards achieving a certain goal, once they understand that, they give you, the teacher, their support and we can all work towards that goal.'

He knows that his recent success has directly encouraged his students, opening their eyes to possibility; and not just them but the wider community too.

'And now I am in more of a position of influence, people see this and it changes things.'

Peter makes weekend home visits to those students who may need a little extra help and support. Like many, they often live in one room with the rest of their family or share a space with other families so there is little privacy or quiet for study. He knows we see the hardship of this 'because of what we can compare it to but for them, they are okay, they are organised and happy and this is what they know'. What is difficult to witness is the lack of food, water, clothing, lighting and learning materials, all basic requirements that every child should have regardless of the life they have been born into. It is so hard for parents and children to prioritise school when they are preoccupied with where their next meal is coming from. Peter says they see the value of education but 'their most important thing is accessing money. And food. That is it.'

Times are changing though, and the younger generation knows education is their best chance, not just to survive but to thrive. Peter is relentless in his pursuit to get more girls into the classroom too. School can be considered a waste of time for girls as they may be married off at sixteen, so changing this mindset has been one of his main priorities. In the last few years his hard work has paid off, with girls leading over boys in the four annual school tests, but he acknowledges there is more still to be done within the tribal cultures.

'So much of it is about money and the bride price that a groom is expected to pay, whether in cattle, property or cash. It's a tradition that's hard to break. This is often why parents don't give priority to their daughters' education.'

Asking Peter what his proudest achievement is makes him squirm. He is incredibly humble and uncomfortable talking about himself, so he immediately redirects the question to encompass the success of his students and how they have navigated through the recent pandemic. Those who have moved on to higher education are now mixing with students from more privileged backgrounds and well-resourced schools, and yet Peter's alumni are just as competent and qualified to be there. This is what makes him smile, a broad, bright smile that radiates joy.

'When I see my students at college or competing at national and international levels in competitions and I see them succeeding, I reflect on where they have come from and what is achievable. To me, it's such a great result, it gives me hope that what I am doing is not in vain.'

It doesn't mean there isn't failure. Peter talks of one student, Mary, who worked hard with a team on a science project and was devastated when they qualified for the international championship but there were no funds to support them to attend. It was a hard lesson to learn, particularly as the following year their contemporaries did gain financial help to get them to the USA, as she stood by and watched.

'I told Mary no, this is not the end of it. And I think she listened and worked hard, even if she was disappointed. A year later she and her team had an opportunity to go to America and they showcased their project to med schools and institutions. They were mentored on how to give a presentation and they became better than me, which is what I am for, what I support, that someone achieves and then becomes better than yourself. And Mary didn't give up. She is in the USA right now on a scholarship and she sends me her grades, they are the top grades.'

Spending time with Peter, I am reminded of the adage of triumph over adversity, both for him and for those who have been lucky enough to be taught by him, and I wonder what they would say about him? I tell him I know this is a hard question for him to answer.

'Maybe that I am teaching them to be confident and curious? And how to approach people. Use your power for the benefit of others too. It's about self-belief and humanity despite the challenges we have all faced growing up in poverty, it doesn't mean an end, they are going to succeed and life is going to change.'

It's clear how valued Peter is by present and past alumni and how every update from his old students is a boost.

'I can see a big transformation, from when they started school to where are now. And even better, they challenged me. It's quite encouraging.'

The master of the understatement.

There is a long list of people who have shaped and influenced the man Peter is today, but he singles out three. The first is his father, who brought him up to take his studies seriously but also to learn how to live with people and respect them, to be a good Christian.

'He instilled in me a value system that my holistic approach to education stems from. If someone comes to me for food, you give them food today and then tomorrow they are hungry and so you look at the long term, you look at the future of this person and these children.'

He says the second inspiration was the Kenyan activist Professor Wangari Maathai, the first African woman to win the Nobel Peace Prize, in 2004.

'I felt like, oh, if someone can emerge from my kind of environment and they are able to share globally, maybe one day I can make something happen.'

Nelson Mandela is his third great influence, particularly because of the personal sacrifice he made for the sake of others. This resonates hugely with Peter. He believes putting others first and sharing what you have makes people scared of what they could lose, but if they can take the risk it will make them happier, harmonious people.

'They always ask themselves, what am I going to get from this? What am I going to get? They are trying to come up with strategies on ways to benefit themselves but what if we thought about others? It could make the world a better, more peaceful place.'

The word 'inspire' comes from Latin, meaning to breathe in, and I think this is incredibly apt for Peter. He creates an air, a life force, for his students to live in and grow. I think that's the most extraordinary thing about him and how this positivity and enthusiasm rubs off on all who meet him. He refuses to ever give up even when faced with the most challenging students and situations.

'Never surrender. Keep looking for the best solution on how to give support. Sometimes I have to think of other creative ways to engage them and then I see change. It's not just about being the teacher you were trained to be but to continually step beyond it. It's hard, of course it is, and it can double your workload, but we must keep thinking of a way forward and listening to the ideas of the people around us.'

Esther Wojcicki

82, Palo Alto, USA

'Let your children play after school. Stop signing them up for so many extracurricular things and give them the opportunity to play because my theory is that play is like research for kids. A way of learning about the world'

Esther Wojcicki is a leading American teacher, journalist, author and mother of three grown-up daughters, who has written a bestselling book on parenting, *How to Raise Successful People: Simple Lessons for Radical Results*. A pioneering powerhouse in education, Esther dared to be different, and continues to push boundaries and look for alternatives to traditional teaching. She is my kind of woman.

Esther was born in New York City in 1941 to Russian Jewish immigrant parents, and was the first in her family to go to university. She studied English and political science at the University of California at Berkeley, gaining a double major degree, and went on to achieve a Master's in journalism. Her heart was set on becoming a journalist.

'That was my goal. It was very difficult for women in the 1970s to get jobs as journalists because the profession was male-dominated. I couldn't even get into the San Francisco press club because I was a woman. I couldn't do a lot of things because I was a woman.'

In those days, she says matter-of-factly, a woman's job was to get married and have kids, so that is what she did; and she decided that if she couldn't be a journalist, she would teach it instead. She got a job at Palo Alto High School as an English, maths and journalism teacher and was quickly surprised to see that her own method of teaching – which was less hierarchal than the norm and where the students were allowed to be as expressive as they wanted – was a success. Or at least it was for the students and for her; less so for the school.

The administration turned up to Esther's class one day, before she had tenure and was still on probation – it was standard procedure to watch and evaluate the new teacher. They were horrified.

'They said, I don't know what you are doing in this class but you're not teaching anything. The students should not be talking to each other. The whole thing was awful. They threatened me with the sack and gave me two weeks to turn it around.'

Esther was traumatised by the experience and her husband told her to quit, but she had other ideas.

'So, I confessed to my students. I told them what was happening, that this was a non-traditional class and that my methods were unusual and if they wanted it to continue they needed to cooperate with me. We had to pull back on the open discussions when we were being observed.'

When the administration returned a fortnight later they were stunned to see a classroom of silent students.

'They came back several days in a row because they couldn't believe it. They said what did you do to the kids? I wasn't going to tell them. And so I passed.'

This story touches me deeply. Not only that the students cared enough about Esther to protect her but also that she reached out to them and asked for their help. She was honest and they responded to that.

'When I realised I could work with them, that was a huge moment.

You guide, you coach, but they don't have to follow your every rule. In fact I have them create the rules with me.'

The journalism programme Esther ran at the school started with twenty students. The following year the enrolment doubled as the word spread. She realised the reason the students liked the class was because she gave them power and control.

'It was all about relationships. And I treated them as equals, which shocked the daylights out of them I think! Don't forget this was in the 1970s and 80s, and no teacher behaved like I did.'

I am keen to know what that looked like back then and how Esther afforded her students that sense of control while keeping the structure of the class?

'Instead of me lecturing all the time, I gave them the opportunity to work together in groups and so they were working with their friends and we all had a common goal. I think it made a difference to them because then they wanted to be there. The goal wasn't just my goal, it became theirs and something they wanted to achieve.'

This reminds me of the conversation I had with fellow teacher Peter Tabichi (page 83) about how a shared motivation empowers everyone involved. I can see how powerful this educational approach is, but what else did Esther have up her sleeve?

'I think I have a kind of quirky personality, I like humour. And I really liked the kids, it wasn't just a fake thing.'

The combination of Esther respecting them, giving them control and focusing on those relationships made a difference, even at that time, before she had really understood what she was doing as a teacher.

'I realised something too, something really important, which is kids don't learn when they are sad and miserable. I think the majority in the school system today are miserable and they are learning because of fear, or because they are doing what they are told, but not because they understand the importance of studying.'

This is such a simple but impactful consideration.

Esther's journalism class was always held on the last period, and the students didn't want to go home when the bell rang. This makes me laugh out loud – students wanting to stay on at school when they don't have to?! It's a rare thing. Esther found it funny too, and reassuring as a teacher, but as the programme grew bigger she had a huge battle with the administration. She had successfully bucked the system and was not following the standard protocols of the teacher/pupil relationship.

'If you came into my class you would see chaos. I mean, kids running everywhere, working together. Also, I did something that was somewhat against the school rules. When the students stayed later, I bought them food. You know, they were hungry. And so that also became part of the culture of the programme.'

Even though Esther wanted to go home at the end of the day, she was excited about being there with them. The programme went from strength to strength and now has over 700 students, six journalism teachers and a designated 25,000-square foot building – the Media Art Centre – that the city of Palo Alto built for the programme she founded. She is still in slight shock and much delight at this, over a decade later.

The journalism programme Esther ran took a professional approach. As each assignment was turned in, the students were then given notes and the opportunity to revise their work.

'I never gave them grades until their final revision. And the final revision meant if it was "publishable". If it's publishable, it's an A, if it isn't publishable, well then you just have to work on it till it is.'

Esther also encouraged peer-to-peer learning, where the students read each other's work and commented.

'I was just the coach. And I said to them, no one writes it perfectly the first time. I told them about being a young reporter and being revised constantly.'

As an art teacher I take a similar view. I want my students to see how much work I put into something and understand this is what we all do, whoever we are and whatever stage we are at.

After teaching at the same school for forty years, Esther retired in June 2020.

'Not because I wanted to but because of the pandemic. My theory was that the virus was not going away any time soon, even though people said it would be over in a month or two. I taught for the first few months but I could sense I was being controlled by the administration and I didn't want to be in that situation. Stopping then was probably the smartest decision I ever made.'

Esther may have left teaching but she remains in education; she has founded an EdTech company with a former student: teach.track. app, an online, project-based learning platform for children aged eight and up. Teachers and parents (if they register as 'families') can sign up for free.

'We have thousands of kids and teachers involved and the goal is to give students the opportunity to pick what they want to do. So the teacher sets it up and the kids work together in teams. I wanted to recreate the culture of my classroom online.'

I can see the appeal of freeing up the teacher for a lesson and giving the students a taste of control, but I can also see the pitfalls. As an art teacher I am used to encouraging independent work, but it's a difficult concept to imagine in other areas of the school.

'This programme I have devised fits into the traditional school structure, it isn't instead of it but, for twenty per cent of the time, it gives students the control. It's created by kids from fifteen to twenty-two for those aged eight to fourteen, so the idea is to have younger kids being engaged because older kids are involved, and there's no one more powerful for a child than another one who is a little older.'

One of the issues Esther has championed throughout her esteemed career is how to make children feel better about themselves. Addressing this, she believes, will help them avoid addiction and a myriad of problems as adults. She is also passionate about misdiagnosis around ADD and ADHD.

'A child's natural desire is to run around, be individual and explore. At school, we try to control it and that causes problems and potentially leads to an inaccurate diagnosis. Particularly in boys, who are biologically more likely to be physical. I think we should be focusing on making kids feel good about themselves and teaching them how to learn and how to cope with adversity. And I think we don't do it. Sorry. It's not you and me. It's the system.'

It's clear what sort of impact Esther has had on her students, but who has had the biggest impact on her? It is an impossible question; she says there are many, but she does single one out, a boy who was struggling. He almost didn't get into Esther's journalism programme because of literacy issues, and then his timetable ruled him out, but he still wanted to take the class.

'I thought what the heck. So I said, look we will do a tutorial one to one. It took a lot of my time but then he was able to join my regular class. He worked really hard and did so well, he wasn't a natural writer or socially adept – he was very short for his age too – and when he ran for editor of the programme and didn't get it he was devastated. But he kept going. And the thing that impressed me the most about this kid was that, because I believed in him, that made him believe in himself.'

He devoted himself to the programme even though he wasn't editor, before telling Esther that he was going to apply for Harvard, asking her to write his recommendation.

'I thought, are you nuts?! I agreed and I wrote but I told them the truth. I am not one of these teachers who glosses over things. I said this kid didn't get to his goal but he worked anyway and became an outstanding student reporter and a leader in the class even though he didn't have the title. He wasn't editor. And I was sure he was going to be rejected. He was accepted. And it turned out that it was because of the letter, because I said he worked so hard even though he didn't get the title. Today he is a senior editor at a major news magazine. And he grew tall.'

The moral of this story is hard work and belief in yourself. It's that simple. It also important to find an adult who believes in you – Esther was a true friend to this student, and thousands of others too.

As a mother of three high-achieving daughters, Esther has expertly navigated her way through motherhood as well as education. She has written a parental guide to help the rest of us, and devised a useful code with the acronym TRICK – which stands for Trust, Respect, Independence, Collaboration and Kindness.

'I created that acronym to help people remember what I think is important and can apply to all aspects of life – parenting, home, schools, workplace. Children, your partner, your colleagues, they want to be trusted and respected, given a lot of independence. They don't want to be dictated to so collaborate with them, and treat them with kindness. I think kindness is so easy to do, and people just don't do it. Kindness can even be just saying good morning, smiling. So, anyway, that's my message to the world.'

And more directly to parents?

'Let your children play after school. Stop signing them up for so many extracurricular things and give them the opportunity to play because my theory is that play is like research for kids. A way of learning about the world.'

Esther recoils at the thought of helicopter parenting and the amount a child is controlled, even for all the loving, noble reasons of protection and growth. I am aware that I have issues with control and my children have much less freedom than I did at their age. Esther tells a story about looking after her grandchildren one Saturday and dropping the older two (who were nine and ten years old at the time) at Target, a big department store, so they could shop while she took the younger one for a haircut.

'I thought they would just phone me when they were done. It's a big store, it was pretty safe. And my daughter called and asked how the day was going and I explained what I had done and she was like What?! WHAT?! I could hear she was hyperventilating.'

Esther went straight back and picked the children up. They were fine; in fact they were more than fine.

'They loved it. And they were so proud of themselves. Then I put that story in my book and so many people related to it because they were afraid to let their kids do anything by themselves. They were so scared something awful would happen to them.' It is about finding the balance between today's world and the relentless newsfeeds, and allowing children more freedom.

That said, it is impossible to ignore one of the main news stories of our recent times, the pandemic, and how this has impacted on children globally. From an educational perspective Esther has a positive message.

'So every student who has missed school feels like they've lost something, and indeed they have, it's called learning loss. But they also learned other things and they need to recognise that and the adversity they managed to overcome. Instead they are trying to catch up by memorising information and the research shows that you forget about eighty per cent of that within a year.'

Esther shrugs. She has been thinking about how this issue can be addressed before we end up with a lockdown generation of deeply troubled adults, and I trust her indefatigable spirit and brilliant revolutionary approach. Esther is a true maverick and a very welcome one.

Shi Wang

50, Beijing, China

'Do not tell your children they are the best. How can you define best? Of course, you should encourage them, be patient, respect them as individuals, but do not tell them they are the best. It puts too much pressure on them or it makes them believe they really are better than everyone else'

Shi taught English for over twenty years at the globally renowned Beijing No. 4 High School in China. Considered the best school in the country, it organises student exchanges between other high-performing schools, including Eton in the UK, and, of the students who choose to study abroad, over ninety per cent go to American universities. The words of the school's first principal, Wang Daoyuan, are inscribed on a sculpture, urging students to 'stand on your own feet, and to advocate and follow moral behaviours. It is your knowledge base rather than others' power that will help you the most. Now you are in your best ages, and you are dreaming big. Will you choose to be people who will make great contribution to the community and society?' These loosely translated sentiments are echoed by Shi and reflected in the educator he is today.

In his second year of teaching at No. 4, Shi was sent to America, to an affiliated school in Massachusetts with several students, before travelling across the country from 'east to west and north to south', visiting all the big universities. People expected him to spend much of his trip in libraries, focused on academic learning, but he was hungry for cultural experience and language practice. As well as supporting those who wished to apply to international universities, Shi also accompanied students to the summer school at Eton. This led to an innovative change of direction, and he became one of the first professional counsellors at a Chinese public school to offer college admission counselling for students. Shi is now founding principal of an international school under the umbrella of Tsinghua University High School in Beijing, a respected expert on international education, and has established a nationwide counsellors' association in China. He is a revolutionary of the best sort.

'We didn't care about the students' career path, who they were or what they wanted or needed. We were totally results-driven and focused on perfectionism. Our only benchmark was exams. If you made a mistake you were a loser. Now, changes are happening in education here and we are looking at the individual. It is energising and hopeful.'

There is still a clear divide between the wealthy and the under-privileged in education, with the former spending money on tutors to access the best schools and universities while the latter have very few opportunities.

'It is a kind of legend that students from disadvantaged back-grounds can get into the top universities. It happens once in a blue moon, but we are working hard to tackle this too and attitudes are changing. Students used to only care about themselves but now they are aware of others around them who may need help.'

Shi has found the topic challenging to discuss with those who prefer a traditional approach to blinkered study and achievements. He doesn't want to slow anyone down but nor does he want to leave anyone behind. He is breaking the mould, but new ways of thinking are uncomfortable for people to explore. Luckily, he is able to witness the changes.

'This reminds me of Darren, a student I taught at No. 4. He was the chairman of the student council and very mature; he already seemed middle-aged. He visited Eton with me and then got into Yale University in the USA. He was sensible, clever and popular.'

Darren took film studies at Yale, which included a year in France. When he graduated he was making documentaries in New York, and Shi caught up with him when he was there.

'We had a coffee on Times Square and he told me he was gay. It was a brave conversation in which he was open, honest and relaxed and I was proud of him. He hadn't told his parents but he planned to come home to China and tell them then, which he did. They didn't embrace his orientation initially, but they didn't discourage him either and gradually came around to it.'

A year later, Darren returned and moved between Shanghai and Hong Kong, where he founded a frozen yoghurt chain store and coffee shop and later began to consult for others who are also pursuing entrepreneurship.

'I was so impressed by him. Not just as an entrepreneur but as a person who really understood what he wanted. He respected himself and his choices. He didn't follow the usual banking or corporate route of someone with his elite education, or continue in film-making when he wasn't sure it was for him. Now he is a shop owner and a happy one! We still keep in touch.'

What Darren gained through his schooling was the ability to know who he was and what he wanted. That feels like the biggest achievement of all. Like another of Shi's students, Alex, who also stepped beyond expectations.

'Alex was clever. He went to No. 4, to Eton and then to Harvard

University in the USA. After a year of working at a global management consulting company in Boston, he quit and came back to China. He started doing volunteer work and gained sponsorship to provide iPad technology to students in poor areas of the country.'

Alex saw where resources were needed and he worked to provide them. He is now developing software to help disadvantaged students with mathematics.

'It could have been very different for him but he saw a huge social issue, a problem that he could help to solve. He wanted to take advantage of his background and find a niche to help others. He worked hard and thought logically about how he could be of most use. He approaches things in a smart way.'

Both students followed the customary educational path in China, but once they became men they stepped off the treadmill and embraced their destinies. Shi is leading a fantastic generation of young warriors who use their knowledge and global experiences to benefit society. He shares these stories of success with his current students to inspire them to find their own way, even if it is not what is expected of them. They are the freedom-thinkers.

'You know, people assumed both Darren and Alex would stay overseas but they came back to China. They made their careers and their lives here. The same with one of my female students, Sue, who followed a similar trajectory and then returned to China to work at the Harvard Business Centre in Shanghai on the "China Thinks Big" initiative.'

The competition invites students to work with Harvard professors on problem-solving in cities across the country. They look at creating opportunities and supporting developments as well as addressing issues like sewage in Nanjing, designing a new community space or building a reservoir, for example.

'It teaches them not to just care about their textbooks but to think about the world around them. Sue loves the project research with students and the attention it places on the environment, the community and families. She, like the others, inspires me to continue working in international education because I can see the benefits for these students. They gain a different perspective about their future.'

Shi tells his students they each have their own position in the world, no matter who they are. They are equally important in society; and he is keen to share this message with parents too.

'Do not tell your children they are the best. How can you define best? Of course, you should encourage them, be patient, respect them as individuals, but do not tell them they are the best. It puts too much pressure on them or it makes them believe they really are better than everyone else.'

The reverse of this is the parents who tell their children they are hopeless, who use tough love to galvanise them to work harder. Shi is infuriated by this.

'This approach does not work either. It doesn't make sense. In China, we seem to swing from one to the other – either the child is on a pedestal or is told they will never be able to climb onto it. Instead we need to remember each student is different, not better or worse.'

When Shi talks about his students, his face lights up. He says they keep him current. Like Ben, who is studying music engineering at New York University. Ben had always been interested in music, particularly beatboxing and rap. When Shi had an idea for his school he knew just who to call.

'I wanted to make a video that would reassure students applying to college, so I wrote some lyrics for a rap to accompany it and called Ben. I wanted him to put music to it and help me with the film. My daughter thought it was hilarious. She prefers classical music anyway, but I like rap.'

With his former student's experience and support, Shi could make something that would inspire his current students. He finds this one of the most satisfying parts of his work, with one generation leading the next. From our conversation there is one sentence that will remain with me.

'You know, young people, they own the world.'

And they do, and I just hope we are on the right track in how we equip and empower them to step into the future.

Miriam Manderson

50, London, UK

'As a teacher, I am in the game of getting young minds to believe they can become something'

Miriam was raised on the notorious Stonebridge Estate in north-west London. Well known for its high rates of crime, it was a difficult backdrop from which to imagine a bright future, but Miriam was determined and driven. From nowhere, she found a passion for languages, which was encouraged by her French teacher. Following a degree in languages, Miriam combined her interest in working with children with her aptitude for French and Spanish. She became a teacher almost thirty years ago.

'That was it for me. I had found what I enjoyed doing and was good at. I later made the decision to continue my teaching journey in a school with challenging circumstances because I wanted to give back to my community. It was walking distance from where I lived.'

The all-boys' school where Miriam started was a tough place to start as a newly qualified teacher, but she had a wonderful mentor – a flamboyant male French teacher – who encouraged her to experiment and be free in her approach. She watched him transform a class of disaffected teenage boys from deprived backgrounds into a group who stood straight-backed and proud, singing songs in French. He got them where he wanted them to be. It was like a magic trick that Miriam wanted to know the secret to.

'I saw several teachers who achieved similar results, like the history teacher who had them in the palm of her hand. She never raised her voice once. She was fair and consistent and they trusted her. There was a young boy in the school, Dwayne, who was disruptive and difficult to teach. He would do his utmost to turn every class upside down, but not history. There he was a completely different child and had a respectful relationship with his teacher.'

This was one of Miriam's first and most powerful lessons while she was training. It taught her not only about consistency but also the importance of connecting with her students on a personal level, showing a genuine interest in them as individuals without being intrusive. She also saw how important it was to display real passion for the subject she was teaching. Miriam took these gems of educational wisdom on to her next school, which had just been turned into an academy.

'The first of the schools that were changed into academies were because of behaviour issues. So, this was where I really cut the mustard and when I really became a teacher. It took all my skills and my background to conquer this. I invested a lot of time, in and after school, talking to the students about why the world saw them in a certain way and how they needed education to change these blinkered views.'

Miriam's students responded to this approach because, for the first time, they didn't feel someone was scolding them. She knew if she nagged them they would switch off. Instead she made them feel valuable and gave them a sense of belonging in their school and community. Much of this work was achieved in the after-school catch-up sessions Miriam ran.

'I would speak to them about their day, why they may have got into trouble with a teacher, who was at home for them, what they would eat if their parents weren't there and how they would spend their evening. At six o'clock we would leave the school and walk home together. I called myself the community mother and I kept an eye on them in the street, not just in the school.'

One of the most important early experiences Miriam had, as a teacher and as a Black woman, was in the classroom with a blond, blue-eyed boy called David. He was incredibly attentive throughout the lesson but there was also something perplexing him. Miriam asked him what was wrong.

'He said, Miss, you teach French but you're Black? And I said yes, and let's have a look at all the countries in the world that speak French. These students hadn't ever seen a map of the world and they definitely didn't know which languages were spoken nor where in the world. My lesson just evolved. David eventually got over his shock, he was a brilliant student to teach.'

Not only had Miriam bridged the gap between how she looked and what she taught but she also made it clear that her fondness of languages did not come from a childhood of privileged foreign trips. She had a similar background to many of the underprivileged students in her class and she knew it was important to be open about this.

'As a teacher, I am in the game of getting young minds to believe they can become something. Most of these children did not have the opportunities the more affluent and privileged have, but I wanted them to know it didn't make them any less of a being. I had been where they were and I had fallen in love with the French language without ever going there on holiday.'

For all the students who thrived under Miriam's care, there are those who were too hard to reach, including a few who sadly passed away in gang-related incidents. This weighs heavily on her shoulders and has shaped her as teacher and mother. At one time, Miriam's husband worked for the campaign Not Another Drop, which meant 'Not another drop of blood, please, we're sick and tired of the knife crime'. They organised a march and the local newspaper ran a story on it, including photographs of recent young victims. Several of the faces in the article had been Miriam's students or at her school and others had been convicted for knife-related offences.

'I had one student, Ricardo, who I taught for five years. He was very sweet but he wasn't very able and he was incredibly self-conscious. I tried to find a way to support him without singling him out and causing him shame and embarrassment. I wanted him to keep trying but whatever I did, it wasn't enough. It didn't save him from peer pressure or a judgemental society, or give him tools and skills to survive beyond his own four walls. He couldn't see there were other ways of living life. He was barely an adult when he was convicted of murder. It was heartbreaking.'

One of the common links between those students who struggled was when one or both parents were absent for long periods of time for various reasons, including returning to their native countries.

'I could instantly tell when parents were not around by the way the children smelled, how they looked, whether they'd had enough sleep or if their uniform was clean. They were dishevelled and there was nobody protecting or nurturing them at the beginning and end of each day. Ricardo was one of these children. Outside school he was left to his own devices and made terrible choices.'

Alonso, another of Miriam's students, had a similar background to Ricardo – with two big differences. The first was that even though his mother was absent for periods of time, she was still very much part of her son's life. The second was his early upbringing in Jamaica.

'Alonso was at primary school in Jamaica before he moved to London as a high school student. There they are taught to respect the teacher and the importance of education, so he couldn't believe his UK peers didn't feel the same. He was vocal about this in lessons and would tell his classmates to shut up because the teacher was talking. This was in complete contrast to Ricardo, who had been brought up to think it was cool to disrespect teachers, be anti-education and hide your deficiencies.'

Ricardo ended up in prison. Alonso is a chef at a top London hotel. Then there was Nadege. Miriam taught at a school in south London for over ten years and achieved language college status there. Miriam says she does not have favourites in the classroom, but it is clear there was a mutual respect and appreciation between her and French-speaker Nadege.

'I like to call her my protégé. She loves languages as I do and is now fluent in Spanish as well as her native French. As her teacher, I felt like I had planted a seed and instilled a passion and enthusiasm for something that informed her future and continues to fill her with joy. She became a teacher, a mother and now she heads up the language college I started. We keep in touch and I am so filled with pride!'

Miriam will not take any credit for Nadege's career choice but I am sure, if I asked Nadege, she would give credit to her teacher.

'I was surprised when she told me she was doing her PGCE. I don't think she planned to become a teacher but she had been happy at school. She used to contribute in class, and helped those children who struggled with French. I have taught children who had shame in having a native language, so I would work hard to make them see it as an advantage. I want every child to feel a sense of pride about the language they speak. Nadege was a positive example of this.'

I have known teachers feel intimidated by students who have more knowledge than they do or who will challenge them. Not Miriam. She thrives in this type of environment and encourages students to reach their full potential, homing in on the superstars too, like Alex, who Miriam learned the biggest lesson from.

'Alex had come over from the USA and she was good at everything – maths, English, languages, sport – and I think this irritated her peers. Her self-confidence was something to behold. She was also straight-talking, verging on rude when I first met her, and would compare British teachers to their American counterparts. She was used to a collegial way of teaching where there was more facilitation, as opposed to instruction, which she found easier to understand.'

Irritated by her behaviour, her friends, classmates and then the entire year group ignored her.

'They "sent her to Coventry", that old-fashioned term, meaning nobody talked to her. I had never witnessed anything like it. It was in her examination year too, so I was worried about the effect it would have on her. Do you know what? She didn't care! She wasn't even pretending not to care, she really didn't. And I watched as each child began to gravitate back to her. The girl who had instigated the exile in the first place observed this too and by the end of the year, everyone was friends again. I found this incredible, because I don't think you can teach self-esteem.'

Like Miriam, Alex had lost a parent when she was very young

and this gave her an inner strength. Alex taught Miriam about being comfortable in her own skin and confident with who she was. Alex was penalised for excelling at lots of things, rather than celebrated for it. By being ostracised many children would have crumbled and dampened their light to avoid standing out, but not her. She wasn't egotistic either. She just believed in her natural ability and refused to apologise for or hide it. Miriam and Alex have remained in touch and Alex is now pursuing her dream as a professional athlete.

For the last three years, Miriam has been the headteacher of a large comprehensive school in north-west London where almost 40 per cent of the students come from disadvantaged backgrounds. She loves her job but misses being in the classroom.

'When I first became a head, I refused to give up teaching completely and kept a weekly language class. Within a month of being pulled out regularly on school matters, I realised how unfair it was on my students and myself. So now I share a lesson with an excellent colleague of mine. When I am in the classroom it is my sanctuary. Jacket off, sleeves rolled up and getting stuck in. Teachers have to learn how to bring children's curiosity alive and make them ask more questions than you are asking them.'

And what must parents do to help their children? We both agree that being present and involved in their children's lives is crucial. Miriam has witnessed too many times when this hasn't happened and how catastrophic the results can be. Her other piece of advice is to be tech-savvy.

'Please don't let your children run rings around you with technology, even if you have to pretend you understand it. I am a fan of technology but we all know the dangers the younger generations face, so we need to keep a close eye on their engagement with the big online world. Parents are usually the bill-payers, so you can access your children's devices. A lot of unkindness and cruelty can come from online activity and, as parents, we have a duty to help children be responsible with the way they use it and protect them.'

Armand Doucet

43, New Brunswick, Canada

'Every day I put the student at the centre and they get a chance to go up to the next rung on the ladder and any time they take a step back, I am there to bring them up again'

Armand believes we all have a superpower. He says his is to connect with people, and he thinks I have the same ability. We first met at a teaching conference over five years ago. He lives in New Brunswick in Canada and I am in the UK, so we find a sweet spot of time when we can catch up over Zoom. He usually has one or all three of his children climbing over him as we chat, and his home is full of noise and laughter. Every Sunday he and his wife cook a big pot of spaghetti for any family and friends who are around, sometimes feeding twenty-five people.

I am always fascinated by the journey people take into teaching and the decisions they make that shape their career. Armand refers to his as a messy squiggle, rather than a traditional linear approach. The realisation he wanted to be a teacher was less of an epiphany and more of a series of 'aha!' moments. It's a fantastic description that feels more practical to me, like regular reinforcements that he was doing the right thing.

Armand comes from a long line of educators and community workers but dismissed any mention of a future in education for him, other than a spell of youth soccer coaching that led to travelling the world with national youth programmes. He went to university to study kinesiology but swapped to pre-med before realising, as he so brilliantly puts it, 'I couldn't sustain the sight of blood and I had a big phobia around needles', so he switched to history. Academia and a life in books wasn't right either, so he reverted to kinesiology.

I think it's important to show that teaching isn't always a calling, or at least if it was calling Armand wasn't listening. He had what I call 'a popcorn brain' of ideas and thoughts but they were confused, so he got a sales and marketing job at a big corporation and continued to coach sports in his own time for six years.

In 2009, Armand persuaded his company to give him a month off and went to Rwanda and Tanzania with his best friend, whose mother worked on the genocide tribunals in Arusha. He learned a lot about human rights, diversity, inclusion and equality on the trip and this inspired him to organise a visit to South Africa the following year (which also fortuitously coincided with the FIFA World Cup). There were two 'aha' moments that followed. The first was on Robben Island where he discovered more about his hero, Nelson Mandela, a man who had unerring faith in his values and strove towards them. The second transformative incident was back at home when a family friend, a teacher, sat him down.

'She said, Armand you really need to think about education, we could use you. She told me what she thought my strengths and weaknesses were and what the education system was going through at that time. It was just a conversation, like so many before, but this time I listened. I think I'm meant for education. I want to try and leave the best legacy I can.'

In the ten plus years Armand has been teaching, he has reached a global audience with his dynamic creativity and heartfelt commitment to his role and his students. He credits them as being the driving force behind everything he does, along with his own children. One of the initiatives Armand started in his first school, that fills me with magical joy, is the Harry Potter programme, where he transformed the place into Hogwarts. For an entire week the teachers were in character – he was Dumbledore – and every lesson was tied in with the book and linked to the curriculum. It took a hundred hours over six months, and then a four-day weekend, to organise and to turn the school into Hogwarts, including the infamous Great Hall, where electric candles were hung to make it look like they floated.

'You want to talk about creativity? Now that was creative.'

They had over 1.8 million views on Reddit and the pupils loved it, rushing home to share their knowledge about owl pellets over the dinner table. Parents were astounded that their children were up early and desperate to get to school.

When Armand moved from middle school, he missed the collegial collaboration. Teaching at high school, with its standardised testing, was a leap but it's a place where he feels he can do good work.

'You know me, Andria, I always say I will sleep when I am dead.'

His focus is on the education system, students, parents and the reputation of the teaching profession. It's a lot to take on but if anyone can, it's Armand.

'Public education is really important. I've been fighting that battle globally because I think everybody deserves that. We need to reform public education to make sure that it's equitable and inclusive, and that everybody has access to these networks and these platforms that can really let them thrive. If that means I need to pay an extra two per cent in taxes, so everybody's all right, then so be it.'

Armand talks about teaching being a fight. I have never thought of it this way but he's right, it is a fight, not just to make sure the kids we teach can find and use their voice but also for the perception of what teachers do. Armand says part of that issue is us, the teachers, and understanding that today's media and communications is a two-way street. He quotes the Irish author George Bernard Shaw, 'the single biggest problem in communication is the illusion that it has taken place', and it's as resonant now as it was when Shaw said it.

'I think part of the issue is that we haven't defended teaching as a proper profession. And I think it's been patriarchal in terms of the management, but consists of eighty per cent women. We need to rise up and start raising our voices that this is a profession, not an occupation, not anybody from off the street can do this job.'

Armand believes we need to be better engaged with the parents and carers of our students too. There is immense pressure for parents these days, whatever the family set-up looks like. Most parents work and feel guilty about how much time they are giving their children and whether they really know what is going on in their heads. It is a guilt I share as the mother of two girls, so I can see the issue from both sides. Armand believes this is a conundrum that teachers need to navigate because reaching out to parents and understanding the battles they face can help us teach and parent in harmony. Which brings us on to the role we play.

'It's an honour to be a teacher. I hate using terminology like "sage on the stage" or "facilitator". Of course, we are many things within that role – a chief and cheerleader for the student, the family, the community – and we are continually communicating those things. In the middle of it all is the most precious commodity, time. To give somebody your time wholeheartedly, it is showing that you care and that you are validating that person is important, right? How many of these kids have that at home, with their parents?'

Asking Armand what he feels has been his greatest achievement in teaching is a question that stumps him for a moment. He doesn't mention the international work he has done or the awards he has won; the biggest impact for him is seeing his students thrive on a day-to-day basis and being part of that process.

'Every day I put the student at the centre and they get a chance to go up to the next rung on the ladder and any time they take a step back, I am there to bring them back up again. I think the greatest achievement is those little wins and I don't think teachers realise how often they do that.'

The downside of this daily journey is the opportunity that may be missed. For all the success stories, there are those who didn't get to where they could or should have, and as their teachers we can take this very personally. Every teacher will have at least one story to share about the student that got away. Armand remembers when he was coaching in the early days – when he was still learning what it meant to teach – and there was a boy who was always jovial and tried hard but came from a difficult background.

'I was aware Brad had family problems and had been moved around various foster homes. One day he just stopped coming. It turned out his new foster-carers had refused to drive him to the training sessions. Had I been more experienced I would have figured out a way to keep Brad, maybe sorted out car lifts. I would have understood just what a vital lifeline the sessions were for him, but I didn't see it and he disappeared. Ten years later I found out he was in jail for murder. He lost his way. I am not saying I could have saved him, but I often wonder if I could have helped him.'

This is a hard story to hear but an even harder story to tell, and I know how much it haunts him. Armand is a perfectionist but he cannot control the decisions others make. He needs to remember all those he has helped and the impact he has made on them. How would they describe Armand?

'Oh, they would say I am completely nuts! I think they would also say he does what he needs to do to reach us. And that I care. I often put their emotional needs first before we deal with anything else.'

Armand is an advocate of the Maslow Hierarchy of Needs, where 'we must take care of emotions before anybody is going to learn anything', and believes this approach is part of the future of teaching. So, if he could share one piece of advice what would it be?

'There was a great band in Canada – the Tragically Hip – and they had a song called "Ahead by a Century" and the lyrics are about life not being a dress rehearsal. And it's precious. And every day I ask myself if I am making the most of my day.'

Hiba Ballout

36, Beirut, Lebanon

'I am inspired by my students as much as I inspire them; it's that circle of inspiration'

The first time I met Hiba Ballout was at the Global Teacher Prize back in 2018. There were around a hundred of us in the auditorium, waiting during an interval for the next presentation, when a woman in a hijab spontaneously stood up and sang the most beautiful song in Arabic. It was Hiba, one of the fifty finalists. Her voice and the confidence she showed in a room full of strangers were amazing and we were all spellbound. We have kept in touch ever since and, as different as our worlds are, there are so many levels we connect on.

When Hiba started teaching science to her primary-age students at St Georges School in Beirut, she was a breath of fresh air, changing the traditional approach to learning by making it more fun.

'Why not play, why not analyse, interpret and just forget about memorising things, other than important definitions. By the end of the year, I had the majority of students liking science.'

This response to her teaching emboldened Hiba to go further.

'I had this way into the hearts of the students, so I thought, why not teach them something beyond science and biology? Why not teach them life skills?'

Hiba, by now the science coordinator at her school, also started managing leadership programmes like Model United Nations and

Model Arab League locally and internationally, and engaged her students in both, giving them an insight into global citizenship. Today she is a hugely respected figure in education, assistant manager and head of the secondary cycle at her school and, above all, a friend to her students. Her fantastic leadership programmes are back after being pending due to the struggles her beloved country is passing through.

One of those paused programmes, Alwan – organised by the ADYAN Foundation – tackles coexistence. Acutely aware of the issues with sectarianism as she is, it is a subject close to Hiba's heart. She remembers such great diversity in schools at the beginning of her career.

'We had Muslims, Christians, atheists and so on and there was an interaction between us. We like living together in the school. And the administration had this idea that we educators, despite our religion, or our beliefs, we have a common message in order to educate these students.'

Now she sees the segregation chasm widening, not just in schools but in communities too, and knows how important and essential the coexistence programme is, not only to her school but also to Lebanon.

'We do not teach religion at high school because it's really personal to the students, and they have the choice to be whatever they want. In the Arab world, it's not so easy to choose what religion you want, because we've been raised on that faith, but when you start reading about other religions, you start cherishing the beauty of each and every one of them.'

Teaching was a dream come true for Hiba. She was born in Saudi Arabia and spent her childhood there with her parents, who had fled Lebanon during the civil war. Her nursery memories were tied up with an Indian-British teacher, Mrs Prema, who the children affectionately called 'aunty'. Hiba adored her and would mimic her at home, adopting her Indian accent when she spoke English and making her older brothers pretend to be her students.

As she grew up, she continued to embrace learning and became interested in biology in secondary school before studying it at university. While her parents hoped she would train to be a doctor – 'you know how parents shape your dreams' – Hiba was determined to become a teacher.

'It's my passion. And I believe, I don't know if it's true, that teaching is a talent, you know, rather than a decision that you take, the same as a musician or an artist, it begins with a talent.'

She stood her ground about her career decision. Talking about it now, she says her father wanted the pride of having a doctor daughter and couldn't see that teaching held a similar respect.

'But we teach the doctors of the future! Teachers are the priority.'

I can see this so strongly in Hiba, a vocation for teaching and a steadfast commitment to educating her students in more than science. Sadly, it has been regularly tested.

'It's hard, when students are living through chaotic days, as we pass through wars, the pandemic, the economic crisis and so on, and they are just waiting for the relief, the peaceful moments that they gain from our words. And even though we may not feel that it's safe in the community or our country any more, we have to give them hope. We must spread positivity despite the negativity that is surrounding us. You see corruption in every single corner and you cannot change anything other than the very small community that is the school.'

Hiba focuses on awakening the hope in her students and encouraging them to be the change they need. I am in awe of her resilience and want to know how she continues, often in the face of despair. What is it that creates this power in her?

'It's the belief itself, believing in our duty as messengers of peace and hope. And in my case, I believe that God gives me science and the ability to spread positivity.'

Religion is a theme throughout our conversation and Hiba's faith is the bedrock of her life. She talks about prayer being a communication and how the presence of God brings a peace deep inside her heart, no matter if it is true or not. And I can connect with that, how it takes a certain type of energy and meditation to keep us on track, whatever our beliefs.

'They look to us – the students, the parents, the community itself – they look at us and think maybe we live a different life from the one they are living, or we never make mistakes, you know, but of course we do make mistakes, we are human. I'll give you a very simple example. I was chatting with one of my students and she had an argument with her mother about making her bed before coming to school. I told her I do my own chores – I wash my clothes for example – and she was amazed. I said well of course, I'm a human being like you and I do things that I have to do.'

Hiba is well aware that some students view teachers as superheroes, and their parents use this to their benefit too, asking her to intervene in certain situations. She believes teachers have just as important a role as the parents at home, because when students come to school they are giving their minds and hearts. We teachers are partly responsible for shaping their personalities.

'I have to always be conscious of what I do, and not do, because they are observing me all the time, considering me as their idol.'

Other than recognition for her work, Hiba says her finest, heartfelt achievement is when students message to say they are going to study biology, become a teacher, apply to the college she went to, or even say she made a positive impact in their lives.

'I believe that leaving such a positive mark in the life of the students is a beautiful achievement, so I guess changing lives would win. I am inspired by my students as much as I inspire them; it's that circle of inspiration.'

She recounts the story of one girl, Rama, who she had taught for several years. She was diagnosed with cancer aged sixteen and called Hiba to tell her. It was an incredibly hard time for Rama and her family, but Hiba also struggled after such a long relationship with her and wanted to support her in whatever way she could. They spent time together and Hiba accompanied her to the Children's Cancer Centre. It was tough but also uplifting and positive.

'Rama was really very strong, a survivor. She's now fulfilling all her dreams, after being cured, and studying to be a pilot. I'm so proud of her. Her mother and father asked to meet the people who had raised me, and I introduced them to my parents, which was very emotional.'

I think this story is particularly pertinent because as teachers we often feel it is our job to fix everything, but there are those times when we can't, when it is out of our control, and that is when it hurts; yet we can still be present.

There are various taboo topics in the Arab world that Hiba navigates on a daily basis. As well as religion there are sexuality, equality and gender issues that are difficult to talk about in her culture. She dealt with a situation recently in class when there was bullying around a conversation about homosexuality and religious diversity.

'I told them that accepting something does not mean you have to believe in it. Whatever a person's beliefs or the way they live their life, is their choice. We are all human and our presence should be accepted and respected. Whether we are Muslims, Jews, Christians, straight or not. I am not a Christian and I do not believe what they do but I respect their belief. Religion is not a barrier. We share this planet together.'

Hiba remembers a focus group where there was a mix of religions present and they were discussing coexistence between different faiths in different regions of Lebanon. A student stood up.

'He said, Miss, it's like a maths exercise. No matter how you solve it you will reach the same solution and God is the maths exercise. No matter the way you take, you are going to reach him. I had never thought about religion this way. I just broke into applause when he finished speaking.'

Hiba believes teachers are change-makers and should be encouraging students to dream big, but that it isn't enough to dream without a plan for how to reach the goal. Parents have an important part to play too.

'They need to be good listeners, because parents often don't listen. Especially to adolescents, the age a child becomes their own person. We are all mysterious at that age and we had our secrets too when we were teenagers, so let children open that box to their parents and be friends. Advise rather than get into an argument that has no recommendations or resolutions – it involves being an active and a good listener.'

Hiba knows she was lucky to have this, growing up. As a child, she would come home from school each day and repeat every single thing that had happened to her to her mother. She never felt her mother did not want to listen to her. As an adult, she calls her mother every day, often twice a day.

Hiba says something that deeply resonates, not just to me as a teacher but as a mother. She says, 'Parents must stop dreaming on their children's behalf, let them dream their own dreams.' And I wonder, not for the first time, how guilty I have been of transposing my own ideas of what my students and daughters should want rather than listening more carefully to them? My eldest daughter attends the school I teach at, which must be embarrassing for her at times. Particularly when her peers say to her, 'Oh your mum is so nice, she's so cool' and her experience of me is as her mother with all the realities that relationship entails. Something David Mitchell and I touch on too (page 273).

'My mother sometimes tells me that talking is easy, but action is so much harder. I am not yet a parent so I can only speak as a teacher, but all my students are like my kids and I have around three hundred and thirty of them.'

If I close my eyes I can still see Hiba standing on an empty stage, singing to an auditorium full of entranced strangers.

Mariela Guadagnoli

51, Galvez, Santa Fe

'There are parallels between architecture and teaching. A house with possibilities is like a child with potential and both should be approached with creativity and hope'

Mariela was an architect in the Argentinian capital, Santa Fe, before she was a teacher. She came from a family of educators and so she had assumed this was where her future lay, but initially her passion for architecture was stronger. While she was studying architecture at university one of her lecturers presented the class with a text to share and then discuss. When they had finished reading it he scrunched the page into a ball and threw it away.

'He said this was a bad text that he had been required to give us because it was on the curriculum, but just because he was our teacher, it didn't mean he was always right and we had to think for ourselves.'

Mariela laughs at the memory of this. Not only had her lecturer given her the freedom to come to her own conclusions but he had ignited in her what it meant to be a teacher. When she graduated, she was invited to a primary school to give classes on technology and immediately knew she was where she wanted to be. This was twenty-four years ago and she has no regrets.

'There are parallels between architecture and teaching. A house with possibilities is like a child with potential and both should be approached with creativity and hope. It is also a matter of perspective, another thing I took from my first career to my second.'

I find this such a simple yet fundamental way of looking at the relationship between the child and the teacher.

There is a story that highlights this beautifully. Mariela was invited to work on a community project that combined her knowledge of architecture with her profession as an educator. She and her students were asked to redesign a historic plaza in Santa Fe, which involved the renovation of large murals with different art techniques. Through this project, the children studied a variety of subjects to create a visual story, incorporating the renowned cardiologist and healthcare campaigner, René Favaloro, considered the second greatest Argentinian of all time. Wherever they included him they also painted a tree with hearts, echoing his vocation. There was much excitement around the project and the mayor came to recognise the work they were doing and congratulate them all. There was one very shy child, Matias, whose reaction momentarily took Mariela by surprise.

'After the praise from the mayor, Matias ran over to me and threw his arms around my waist. He hugged me so tightly. He didn't say a word but, in that moment, I could feel how important the whole experience had been to him. His embrace not only said, "We did it!", I think it was also the moment he realised his own worth too.'

As a big believer in educating by example, Mariela knows this is not just the teacher's role but the parents' too.

'We are all educators in our children's lives and parents are the most important part of this. They must encourage their kids in this "project" of life!'

Mariela teaches technology across four schools and each is very different: a specialist school for underprivileged students, a technical

college for thirteen- to nineteen-year-olds, a private Catholic school
and a primary school with a mix of children. She has faced two
defining battles in her career. The first was as a female teacher working
in a technical college full of men. The second was for others to trust
in her methodology because she doesn't use conventional tests but
evaluates through progress. She is confident in this approach because
of the results it achieves. She and her students have won regional
and national awards, as well as commendations for their ground-
breaking projects. Yet she doesn't measure her achievements by
these successes. What motivates her are the responses from those
she teaches, many of whom beg their school principal to let them
join Mariela's class.

'The best feeling is when students have graduated and they tell me
the impact my classes had on them because of the learning process,
and that I taught them to stand up for what they believed in. My class
affected their lives for the better and they remember me with a lot of
love. That is quite something.'

Ignacio was one of these students. He was a clever boy with complicated behavioural problems stemming from his family background.
A couple of years previously, in his early teens, he had been made
to repeat a year of school because he wouldn't take written exams.
Consequently, he was bored, restless and disruptive. Cue Mariela and
her commitment to project-based learning. Ignacio joined her class
and she adapted her evaluation process for him so he could participate,
and within weeks he was engaged in the work.

'We had a specific technical problem to address. The ground
around the school would flood when it rained, so we needed to find a
solution, and one element of the student project was to make paving

stones from recycled materials that had been discarded by society. Ignacio was captivated and came in with a plastic that we could trial.'

During the year Mariela taught Ignacio, she focused on integrating him into school life and inspiring him, often taking him to science fairs with her. She found out that he had felt judged by every teacher and hated his label of 'bad student' but felt powerless to change it.

'When I selected him to represent our school paving-stone project at a science fair he couldn't understand why I had chosen him over forty other students, but he was thrilled. He confessed that he had been about to drop out of school but that the project, and my teaching, had convinced him to stay. I can't tell you how happy this makes me.'

I know exactly how Mariela feels. Ignacio contacted Mariela recently to say he was changing schools from the technical college to a secondary school, which would mean one year less of study. He wanted to reassure her this was a positive decision.

'He said I could count on him, that he hoped my belief in him would continue and he would not let me down.'

Sometimes it's hard for teachers to find an individual's potential but it is our job to keep trying, even when – especially when – the children won't let us in. Mariela persevered with Ignacio and she should be so proud of them both.

'I consider us talent hunters, a description I heard used by another teacher and it really resonates. It is our job to pay attention to the children, to learn from them and to light up their learning. They have open hearts that need to be filled.'

Howard Freed

69, Hertfordshire, UK

*'I have seen the consequences of hardship
through the children I have taught, who had
their whole lives ahead of them, but were victims
of circumstance. It makes those students,
who found a way out to good professions
and happy lives, even more amazing'*

Howard has been in education in London for forty-six years. From an economics teacher, to a headteacher and now a mentor and coach for headteachers, his journey has taken him through diverse communities and schools. He is a voice of expertise, reason and inspiration and I am honoured to call him a friend as well as a valued colleague. He is the godfather of teaching.

'My first job was in 1976 at Reynolds High School in Acton in west London. I didn't know the area at all. It was the first position I was offered, I took it and I just fell in love with teaching.'

In 1984, three local secondary schools were amalgamated into one, including Howard's, and he became part of the senior leadership team of the newly established Acton High School. It took children from the South Acton Estate, one of the most deprived estates in London, where they were growing up in very difficult circumstances, including dire poverty and high suicide rates.

'Many of the children had no background of education in their family. They weren't aspirational. They were challenging, but if you got through to them, they really wanted to learn. The odds were stacked against us, but we managed to get most students through their exams and a good number of them went off to university and on to professional careers including an Ofsted inspector, an engineer and a barrister.'

As well as teaching economics at GCSE (as it is now) and A level, Howard took a pastoral role and became a head of year, dealing with any number of incidents that, on rare occasions, meant calling an ambulance. One moment, Howard would be sorting out a fight between students and the next, those same boys would be united in the football team, proudly playing together for their school.

'They were the sort of children who would drive you to distraction. I know they made some teachers' lives a misery. They were also utterly lovable to many more of us. If your car wouldn't start, they would be fighting each other to push it and help out.'

I am always fascinated to know how teachers build this sort of connection with their students. For Howard, it is simple. He believes if children know that you care about them and you want them to do well, they will respond to this. While bad behaviour on occasions is inevitable, it is the teacher's, and the parents', role to reinforce the boundaries, chastise and, importantly, to forgive.

'I was always on their side and they knew it. Many years ago, I was a witness in court for one of my students. What he had done was wrong and, of course, I was honest about that, but I also wanted to express all the positives of this boy.'

Howard recalls a school trip to Margate. These days out were a huge undertaking for the school, involving five coaches and lots of staff support. Many of the students had never left Acton, or seen the sea before, so this was a definitive moment in their childhood. The students walked around the town and went to the beach, hoping they would be allowed some time in the amusement park. They were all well behaved and the day passed without incident until they got back to the coach.

'A high percentage of our students were from Afro-Caribbean backgrounds. As we got back on the coach, a group of white youngsters gathered and started hurling insults. I could feel the fury rise around me and knew our boys were ready to leap out and give the group a right pasting, so I told the coach drivers to leave immediately. We all talked about it on the way home and the teachers explained why we stopped them responding to the racist taunts. They got it but, under-standably, it was hard for them.'

Howard credits his students with teaching him about resilience. These were disadvantaged children growing up in extreme poverty, surrounded by prejudice.

'They lived in poor-quality tower blocks, caught in the vicious circle of the council accusing residents of not looking after their envi-ronment. This would be used as an excuse not to spend any money on the flats, so nothing was ever made better. And each morning the children would leave these places to come to our school and they would still learn, laugh and have fun.'

Howard is in touch with a good number of his past Acton High and Reynolds High students through social media. The oldest are now in their early sixties but some of them didn't live beyond fifty.

'This is my deepest sadness. They didn't die from addiction or violence, they had cancer or diabetes, illnesses that can be prevalent in poverty. And we are still allowing families to exist like this. I have seen the consequences of hardship through the children I have taught, who had their whole lives ahead of them, but were victims of circumstance. It makes those students, who found a way out to good professions and happy lives, even more amazing.'

For Howard, it has been a huge privilege and pleasure to be a teacher in five schools during his esteemed career, surrounded by inspirational students in each of them. After a decade teaching in Acton, he moved on to a deputy headship in Enfield. The school had many Greek Cypriot children and Howard felt instantly at home. Howard is Jewish and the first parents' evening he attended reminded him of a bar mitzvah, with everyone talking over each other loudly and being tactile. He saw how special it was to have parents who believed in the school and supported his vision for the students. Working within that community was one of the many highlights of his career.

Following this, Howard's first headship was in a tough part of Leytonstone, east London, where he would occasionally have to take baseball bats from the parents or families outside school at the end of the day, let alone the children. The parents or families would arrive in the playground with a gripe against another child or their family, and Howard and the staff displayed a zero-tolerance presence to keep the children safe.

'The school was undersubscribed when I arrived as the new head and we were quite a young staff, but the students believed in us. We became oversubscribed during my headship. One of the most memorable moments there was when one of my great assistant heads wanted to bring in celebrities for our prize-giving events. It was an excellent way to encourage the students. One year he invited Premier League footballer, Ian Wright, who was playing for Arsenal at the time. Amazingly, he accepted. He came into my office for lunch before the awards. The children got wind of this and were climbing the windows and drainpipes outside my office to get a look at him. Ian was fantastic with them all at the event and he left a school full of inspired kids. They will never forget that day.'

After over eight years at Leytonstone, Howard's second and final headship was in Pinner in North Harrow, where he stayed for over thirteen years. It was a more affluent suburb on the outskirts of north-west London. During Howard's headship, the school was high-achieving, increasingly successful and demonstrably inclusive, something that has always been important to Howard.

'We had three boys who, between them, had multiple needs including autism and ADHD. They would always come to see me at break or over lunch, for a chat. The way they navigated their school years was phenomenal. They took part in school activities and productions and the other students and staff were fantastic with them. They went on to take courses at the local college. It was hard to let them go and I wished we had the resources to keep them.'

When Howard joined this school no high school in Harrow had a sixth form. It had been an issue that the local authority had refused to address. Parents in the borough had been campaigning and Howard had been unable to find a solution, until he was on a British Council trip to Poland with the headteachers from five other high schools in Harrow. They were on a train from Warsaw to Krakow when they discussed the problem and agreed a plan of action.

'We shook hands on that train and set the wheels in motion for what was the biggest professional risk of our careers, threatening the financial stability of the schools and, therefore, our jobs and reputations. Over the next couple of years, from 2003 to 2005, we plotted, wrote letters, set up meetings and gained support from parents and governors. In 2006, against the local authorities' wishes, each school set up a sixth form, with an initial recruit of 444 students in total. A hundred and seventeen of them came to the new sixth form in my school. We had no money and were being refused funding. It all looked like it was going to be a disaster. To cut a long, laborious story short, we joined forces with a local college where the principal was brilliant and allowed funding to be routed through her college. Eventually we got everyone on side, including the council. My biggest moment was when those 117 students walked into my school for their first lesson in Year 12. Now there are well over 2,500 sixth-form students across the high schools in Harrow.'

I want to cheer Howard and his colleagues for their patience, commitment and vision. They saw a need and they took risks to fulfil it. Howard is quick to point out that they only succeeded because it was a joint effort between the schools and there was a shared trust. It was about collaboration not competition, something every community should see in their local school network.

'To my embarrassment, when I retired the school insisted on naming the new sixth form block the Howard Freed Sixth Form Centre. I was overwhelmed by that. My biggest regret was that my mum and dad weren't alive to see it. They would have proudly attended the opening ceremony too. My wife and daughters were there, which was lovely.'

As a dad himself, Howard empathises with the guilt that parents carry around. He says we have got to accept it and learn to live with it rather than making it a negative energy. Parenting is imperfect, we are all imperfect. We need to give our children unconditional love but not confuse this with taking away boundaries, because structure is part of the care, not the punishment.

Howard wants all parents to take a real interest in their child's education, but allow the child to say what they want to do, not what you think they should do. Let them make their own mistakes and then help them to recover from those.

'Don't force your background and your experiences onto your child; they are different from you and they have to find their way in life. I think the whole point of parenthood is that your children grow up and can have, as far as possible, happy, fulfilling lives. But that might be very different from your life. And you should accept that, and not judge it.'

Howard is not just a guiding light for young people but for his colleagues too, who he believes need to have the classic teacher combination of self-confidence and humility. One of his key drivers as a headteacher has been the professional development of staff. He is incredibly proud of the thirty or so headteachers who he worked with, either as senior leaders in the two schools he ran or through coaching and mentoring programmes he has led. When Howard speaks, we listen.

Barbara Zielonka

39, Nannestad, Norway

'Everything starts with social emotional learning. We should spend the first few weeks of the school year just focusing on building healthy bonds with our students. Life skills matter so much more than grades'

Barbara was born and raised in Poland. The daughter of two teachers, she knew she wanted to enter the profession from an early age, inspired by observing her parents' devotion to education. When she graduated with a Master's degree, she assumed she would teach in Poland, but a chance encounter with a teacher visiting from Norway changed the course of her life. Not only could she earn more money overseas but it would generate exciting opportunities for her, including travel, which she was passionate about. Aged twenty-five, she left Poland.

For the past fourteen years, Barbara has been teaching English at a high school in Nannestad in eastern Norway, a place that really feels like home to her. The school offers both academic and vocational lines of study including media and communication, sales and service, sports, healthcare and hospitality to their 900 students, some of whom will go on to further education while others will go straight into industry. One of the biggest employers in the area is Oslo International Airport, and the school collaborates with them and other local businesses to establish future routes for their students. Part of Barbara's role is to teach English within an industry setting so students have a practical grasp of the language, preparing them for the workplace.

When Barbara first started teaching she was surprised at the lack of diversity in the first Norwegian school she worked in, with less than 10 per cent of the children coming from elsewhere, mainly Syria, Afghanistan and Sweden. Now her class is sixty per cent Norwegian nationals and the rest are from many other countries and mixed backgrounds. Barbara believes it is vital to build relationships with students as soon as possible to find out who they are, their strengths and what they may need help with. At the beginning of the school year, she catches up with each of her students, and sometimes the responses are unexpected.

'I had a meeting with a student, Mateus, who was fifteen, struggled with severe dyslexia and was troubled by previous bad experiences in English classes. He hated English and he told me he didn't feel like participating in my classes. But what surprised me was when he said I shouldn't spend my precious time on him but should give it to other students who deserved it. He didn't think he was worthy.'

Barbara had been warned about his low capabilities by Mateus's previous teachers, but she took no notice. She says she does not listen to what may be said about a student or how they have been labelled; her job is to come to her own conclusions. In this instance, she knew Mateus needed urgent help and that the answer was to use digital technology, something she advocates strongly for students with educational issues who don't respond to traditional teaching. Barbara began by putting strategies in place that were designed to make Mateus forget about his learning disorder, and introducing him to speech recognition programmes, reading patterns and text-to-speech software.

'I felt like Mateus had spent his school life with "dyslexic" written on his forehead and I wanted to free him from that so he could be open to what I was teaching him. He went from getting a grade 2 – grade 1 being the lowest you can get – to a grade 5 – 6 being the highest. I had seen him go from losing all hope and faith to blossoming with confidence and, while that was my biggest achievement, it was all down to him and his commitment. I will never forget that boy.'

There is a feeling of triumph when you see students benefit from your help, but Barbara and I both know the sense of empowerment we get from working with someone who has given up on themselves. Mateus is now studying electronics at university.

Barbara has the powerful ability to put herself in the shoes of her students and understand what they need. She has huge empathy and believes that everybody can achieve, no matter what their ability or background, if they work hard, show interest and take initiative. This conviction was sorely tested early on in her career.

'I was in my second year of teaching at the high school and a young boy, Ishmael, joined the class. He was the first child I taught who was not Norwegian. He was an orphan who had come from Somalia and been placed with a foster-family. At the time, I didn't know very much about children who came from African countries.'

Ishmael's story was tragic. He had witnessed his parents being shot and had then become a child soldier in Somalia, fighting with a gun bigger and heavier than he was. He arrived in Norway speaking very limited English and no Norwegian, so these factors added to the complex difficulties he already faced.

'He was completely traumatised. In class he was silent, he didn't spend time with children his age or want any kind of attention. I have wooden sticks with the names of my students on and when I need somebody to answer a question, I simply pick one out. Once I selected his name and I read it twice. Ishmael didn't even establish eye contact with me. It was like he was physically in the classroom, but completely absent.'

While Ishmael had been rescued from a terrible life, he had been thrown into a world he had no understanding of. It must have been utterly surreal for him. Barbara was desperate to communicate with him but she didn't know how to.

'I cannot begin to imagine what he thought and felt. I didn't have any reference points or the knowledge to help, so instead I trusted that our welfare system would know how to support him, but they didn't either. Now we are all trained and have strategies and techniques to use but then, no.'

I know how much this haunts Barbara. And how devastating it has been for Ishmael, who could not escape the torment of his childhood and subsequently turned to drugs.

These are the situations that remain with us, and it is easy to dwell on our failures. When Barbara doubts her teaching ability, she reads back over old messages from ex-pupils that remind her why she is doing it. One of these students was Leah. She came to Barbara's class as an accelerated learner, jumping from lower secondary school to high school. She was younger than the other students but she understood the value of hard work, motivation and perseverance.

'To begin with, Leah didn't believe she would be able to get a grade 6 but she took responsibility for her academic progress and was one of the best students I have had in my teaching career. The best part of the story is that she became an English teacher. We are still in regular contact and exchange teaching ideas and resources.'

Barbara lights up when she talks about Leah. She is just one of the many students Barbara has built a supportive and trusting relationship with. I wouldn't be surprised if Leah chose teaching because she was inspired by her mentor.

'Everything starts with social emotional learning. We should spend the first few weeks of the school year just focusing on building healthy bonds with our students. Life skills matter so much more than grades. I don't like measuring performance. Parents shouldn't panic about it either. They need to help their children develop their creativity, dignity and autonomy. Not pay them for every grade 6 they get, which sometimes happens here in Norway. It's a reward for a success but where is their personal growth? We need a reset.'

I share Barbara's views on assessment and how education isn't just about maths and English but should encompass foundation skills. Now more than ever, young people are unable to communicate with others, more used to looking at a screen than a face. Barbara has been a digital technology advocate in the classroom, but I am interested to know how she feels about it generally.

'I am a great fan of digital technology. If you asked me this question ten years ago, I would tell you, it should be used in schools and we can forget about paper, books and handouts. But over the past five years, I have totally altered my perspective. I encourage cellphone-free spaces through community agreements and I have become very selective when it comes to the use of educational apps.'

This is a fundamental change in Barbara's teaching approach. Where she was once encouraging her peers to embrace digital technology, she now sees how much damage it can do if we don't create limits for children and instil screen-free time. One of the messages

Barbara shares with her students is the tyranny of social media and FOMO, the 'fear of missing out'. Instead she talks about the power and release of embracing JOMO, the 'joy of missing out'!

'We adults and parents need to take the lead and do it for ourselves too. I see so many parents in the playground looking at their phones rather than the children in front of them. This is happening everywhere, not just Norway. Children are amazing and we need to find out who they really are by talking to them. If we communicate well with them then they will grow up knowing how to communicate well with others, not just through social media.'

Barbara shares such an important message that, as adults, we cannot ignore. We need to lead by example. Taking breaks from our screens is something we all need to do more. It encourages the children around us to do the same and creates more possibilities for meaningful conversation.

Swaroop Rawal

63, Mumbai, India

'Let your children make some decisions. Or they will get to adulthood and not know how to. Let them choose their career, what to wear, who their friends are and what to eat. Yes, they will make mistakes but it's the decision they took and they will learn from it'

When Swaroop dropped out of college at the age of seventeen, she did not expect to be catapulted into the Bollywood film industry. Although naturally shy, she enjoyed being photographed, and modelling work led to a career in film and theatre. At twenty-one, she was crowned Miss India. She married her film actor partner, Paresh, they had two sons in quick succession and she happily gave up work to be a full-time mother.

When the boys were at school, Swaroop took an active fundraising role in the PTA (Parent Teacher Association) and utilised her theatre skills to run drama summer camps. The classes were a huge success and the children clamoured for more.

'There is no kid in the world who can resist me! This is not me being arrogant, it's just that I love children and they sense it. And they love me back. It's that simple. I have learned that from all the students I have worked with.'

Having spent time with Swaroop, I can vouch for her irresistibility.

While she was on the PTA, the school staff were invited to a course about learning disabilities. Back then, in the late 1990s, this was a largely ignored issue in India. None of the teachers intended to attend, so Swaroop went instead, feeling it would reflect badly on the school if there was no representative. She went to learn.

'Shortly after, my husband saw me reading a really trashy book and he asked why I was wasting my precious time. He was right. He wasn't judging me. Our sons were at school all day and we had staff who helped with the housework, so I had no excuse. I needed to do something for others.'

Swaroop took a Master's in English literature and volunteered at a clinic for children with learning disabilities. She taught drama. In her first class, she had a very mixed group: a slow learner, a girl with speech and language issues (aphasia), a child with hyperactivity disorder and several with undefined learning difficulties.

'In one year, all of them changed. Prisha, the girl with aphasia, was the tiniest in the class but became the bossiest, the "grandmother" of everybody. And Onkar, the slow learner, refused to take a part in the play but wanted to be my assistant instead. On the day of the performance I forgot something and he reminded me. I was so pleased. All I was teaching them were social skills, but it changed their lives.'

At forty, Swaroop did a PhD on the role of drama in enhancing life skills in children with learning disabilities. During her research, she met a child who became very important to her. Salah was eleven, struggled in class and was dismissed by her parents as 'childish'. They openly favoured her brother.

'In my class Salah was like my little puppy. She would always be by my side. Once, I took my additional needs group to the library and when we came out the boys from Salah's class started teasing her. You know the usual stuff about her having to go to "special" classes. I immediately turned around and told the boys she was indeed special and only the loveliest children were allowed to come with me. I just changed the meaning of the word.'

With Swaroop's help, Salah's confidence grew. Around seven years later, Swaroop got a call from Salah. She was working as an intern with one of India's top fashion designers as part of her college course and she invited Swaroop to the fashion show she was helping to organise.

'I arrived and there was a seat for me in the front row. Salah's parents were seated at the back. I mentioned this to her and do you know what she said? She said, "Ma'am, it was you who made the difference." I will never forget this.'

Swaroop believes that many children diagnosed with learning difficulties are of above-average intelligence. In Salah's case, she was severely lacking in confidence and her transformation came from Swaroop believing in her and showing how she could believe in herself.

'You know, we make a big deal about learning maths but when we grow up we use a calculator. As an adult, we write on a computer and use spellcheck. Once these children get beyond school they can find their place in the world. My son has the worst handwriting but he has done his Master's in screenplays and scripts. He just types everything.'

In her PhD, Swaroop wrote that she was going to change the lives of all the children in her country. At the time, she was teaching ten children. I can't help but admire this woman's determination. Those who read her PhD thought her statement was too ambitious and unachievable. Swaroop quotes from one of the holy scriptures in the *Bhagavad Gita*.

'Lord Krishna says you should focus on your goal. Don't worry about failures and successes, just go on doing it because remember you are doing it in his name. I thought, this is great because I am a believer and I knew God was there to help me do it. I also realised that I couldn't achieve my mission by working in one school, I had to think much bigger.'

As well as pledging to work in government schools, Swaroop began training teachers in the state of Gujarat. She reasoned that the more teachers she worked with, the more children she could reach. It was important to her not to give up teaching children either, and so she continued with life skills workshops and training sessions in the classroom.

'I'm probably one of the only teachers in the world who teaches children from preschool to postgraduate. I teach children in nurseries. I teach children who are in child labour and on the street. I teach children who are in elite schools and in government schools. And I'm also teaching postgraduate students too. I travel across the different states of our country and work with the state government, UNICEF and Save the Children. I want to get the child who is working in the fields back into the classroom.'

Swaroop has devised a spiral curriculum with drama at its core, which works from nursery to postgraduate, widening and deepening their reflections as the students age.

'As an example, if we are working on emotions, the younger children will look at good choices and bad choices. When I am with the postgraduates, I am teaching them how one wrong decision can change your life.'

One of the methods Swaroop uses to tackle decision-making and problem-solving is to ask her students to keep a diary. In it they must write down one decision, small or big, that they have made that day and whether it had a good or bad outcome. If it was good, then that was great, but if the result was bad then they had to think of an alternative course of action that could have been taken and note this down. This makes children aware of consequences and gives them the power to learn from their mistakes. Next time they can make a different choice.

Swaroop tells me about one of her university students, Ajay, who was twenty and would fight with everybody in his class to sit next to her. He spent most of the pandemic playing violent computer games and interacting with his friends online. During that time, he told his mates about Swaroop's life skills class and he started teaching them the games she had taught him.

'It helped Ajay and his friends deal with their stress. It gave them a sense of life beyond the pandemic. It was a terrible time for these kids, on the cusp of independence with the fear of how much the world would change.'

Not only did Ajay share the skills Swaroop had instilled in him, he relied on them at a frightening moment in his life. He was in the car with his parents when they had a terrible car accident on the highway. His mother was unconscious but he managed to get her, and his father, out of the vehicle. He remained calm and was able to revive his mother before calling the police and the ambulance.

'Ajay told me he kept it together and walked into the hospital smiling. Then when the doctor helped him, he collapsed. He said throughout the trauma he kept thinking of the problem-solving game I would play with the class and he knew he had to make the right decisions at each point. He managed his emotions and I was so proud of him.'

One of Swaroop's constant battles has been to keep girls in education for as long as possible, similar to Ranjitsinh (page 53). For financial and safety reasons, struggling parents are often keen for their daughters to be engaged by fifteen and married soon after, even though the legal age for marriage is eighteen. Sonal was one of these students. She wanted to continue her studies but her family refused.

'I'm not against marriage, but too young and it prevents young people achieving what they want from their lives. Sonal sat down with her parents and used our problem-solving process as a way to reach out to them. Somehow or other, she convinced them to let her study and now she is going to be a doctor. Isn't that beautiful? Sonal was empowered by the skills I had taught her. She sent me a photo of her wearing her doctor's coat at medical college.'

While Sonal was studying she won a renowned reading prize and was awarded a set of books. She read them all and then she left them at the residential halls where she had been staying.

'I asked Sonal why she had not taken her prize books with her. She said she wanted to leave them for another poor girl to read because there would be another Sonal out there who couldn't afford books. She said I had taught her empathy.'

Books are central to Swaroop's role, first as a mother of two and then as a teacher. She knows the importance of reading to children every day and how crucial this is for those with learning difficulties. Her other piece of advice is about choice.

'Let your children make some decisions. Or they will get to adulthood and not know how to. Let them choose their career, what to wear, who their friends are and what to eat. Yes, they will make mistakes but it's the decision they took and they will learn from it.'

Twenty years after Swaroop made a bold claim in her PhD about reaching every child in her country, she is about to achieve it.

'The government are putting together a new education policy, it's a philosophy. The last one was realised in 1986 so it is about time. They have chosen a hundred people across India to work with them on this and I am one of them. I'm in the group that is writing pedagogy and curriculum. It gives me goosebumps to think that I will be instrumental in setting the curriculum for the children of my country.'

I am thrilled for Swaroop and completely unsurprised by her success. She is passionate about bringing fun back to the classroom and focusing on art and sport too. Not only that but she is keen to raise all students' self-esteem.

'I have witnessed teachers being disrespectful to children, calling them names, labelling them as stupid or lazy. If you tell a child this enough times, they will believe you. It becomes a self-fulfilling prophecy. It makes me so angry.'

Swaroop finds the good in every child and celebrates it. Sometimes she feels she is in the middle of a battle to protect them from a system, or a preconception, but she will continue to fight for them for the rest of her life.

'I have got a pen in one hand and a sword in the other and I will fight for every child.'

Leticia Lyle

41, São Paulo, Brazil

'As a society, we are taught to give answers and come up with conclusions and great ideas, but we aren't taught to ask questions. As parents, we are often guilty of discouraging or ignoring questions, but instead we should encourage children to ask more. If we don't all ask more questions we are going to be stuck with the same answers'

Growing up in Brazil as the daughter of hard-working Italian immigrants, Leticia has experienced both privilege and adversity. When she was nine, her mother took her to volunteer at a community school in a favela (an impoverished urban area). This prompted Leticia to decide she was going to change the world. She wasn't academic at school, but she loved running the student council and organising trips and parties.

'I'm six feet tall, which is literally a giant in Brazil! I had braces and I was very loud. I was full of confidence and highly extrovert. I always believed that every voice counts. What I couldn't understand was why people weren't nicer to each other.'

When Leticia was sixteen, her mother died of cancer. A couple of months later her report card displayed a list of unusually low grades. Leticia felt disappointment in the school system for the first time.

'I remember thinking how unfair this was. I lose my mom and I lose my intelligence? I am just getting myself through the loss of my mother and the school are telling me I am not good enough. I thought, this system is wrong. It should be saying, "You're a winner, you're alive, you didn't fall into drugs." Luckily the teachers I had were really supportive and that's what got me through.'

After studying business, film and law at university, Leticia fulfilled her ambition to become an educational documentary film-maker, committed to showing the world through other people's eyes. She had some success, but she found it frustrating because she did not feel she could reach enough people or make a substantial difference.

'I moved to New York, married an American man and decided to spend some time volunteering on different programmes. Within six weeks I was working a sixty-hour week on a variety of teaching initiatives in low-income communities throughout Harlem and the Bronx. My husband looked at me and said, "When are you going to admit that you want to be a teacher?" It was a dawning moment of realisation.'

Many of Leticia's family are educators, including her aunt, who has taught and lived with the Inuits in the northern territories for the last forty years, and her sister, who created a non-profit that builds libraries in the Amazon. Why had Leticia not thought about teaching before?

'It's a hard profession. Teachers in Brazil are on a very low wage. And if you were clever it was considered a waste to go and work in a school. I have an answer for that now. The best thing I can do with my intelligence is to become a teacher because that is how I can get the most impact out of my brains and my heart. And I can still change the world. That won't happen if I am an executive building PowerPoint presentations.'

At Teachers College, the prestigious education school at Columbia University in New York, Leticia sought a Master's degree in curriculum design and inclusive education.

'I remember sitting in class on my first day there and thinking I had found myself. It was like unicorns were dancing around, sneezing glitter over me and proclaiming my happiness!'

This is a fantastic description of the moment Leticia connected with who she was supposed to be. It didn't make the study any easier; and she was pregnant and juggling a full-time teaching assistant role at a public school, too. The practical teaching experience she was gaining was invaluable, and this is where she learned her first lesson from a student. Alex was in fifth grade, he was twelve and had been diagnosed with autism. He was in a class of children with learning disabilities. When Leticia met him she couldn't see evidence of the disorder. His verbal communication was good, he just had issues with reading and writing.

'I thought he may have been misdiagnosed, but because he had this label he had been treated in a certain way for years, people reading the "label" and not looking at the child. I asked to see his notebook and the teacher said there was nothing in it and rolled her eyes, but in the corner of every page were little drawings and when you flicked through the book they came together as an animation. It was a revelation. When my daughter was born, he gave me his favourite childhood book and inside he wrote, "When you are older, I think you will love this book just as much as I do." It was *Lemony Snicket's A Series of Unfortunate Events*. Alex taught me that students are cluttered with labels and sometimes they are wrong. These are children's lives we are talking about and once they have a label they can be stuck with it for ever.'

Leticia knew she could not be the sort of teacher to toe the line. Like Esther Wojcicki (page 93), her innovative approach and boundless energy have in the past won her many fans but also a few enemies. As a newly graduated teacher in New York, she was full of self-doubt. Eight-year-old Jessica taught her how to trust her gut instinct.

'Jessica was bright but she craved attention and was always trying to make friends the wrong way. By the end of the school year she had made one friend, Nadia, who was sweet but very bossy and loud. She was constantly telling Jessica what to do. In the middle of a lesson, after an articulate altercation, Jessica took her sharp pencil and stabbed Nadia in her hand. I was shocked.'

Jessica was a child who Leticia had been working closely with, and she couldn't imagine where this behaviour had suddenly come from. She sent Nadia to the infirmary and sat Jessica on a chair in the corridor.

'What was as frustrating as the incident was that the rest of the class laughed and it wasn't funny. It was tragic. Jessica was distraught at her behaviour but she refused to say sorry and the class was displaying the same sort of disarray; I was mad and lost at the same time.'

Leticia's colleagues claimed it happened because Leticia was too liberal with her class, her authority was undermined because she was so playful and she had allowed students to come in early so they could dance together before school started. They felt it encouraged unruly behaviour.

'I was a little glittery, I know, but the other teachers used this event as an excuse to point fingers at me. They told me I wasn't strict enough and I started to believe them. I felt horrible. That night I couldn't sleep so I wrote my class a letter.'

In the letter, Leticia said she understood why they had laughed and she had done the same as a child but she didn't like herself for it. Her request was for them all to talk about it and figure out how to move forward. She told them she didn't believe being strict would change the way they acted; instead she needed to work in helping them be more compassionate with each other. The following day she sat down with Jessica.

'She was still defensive, but ready to talk. She said Nadia had been making fun of her and being unkind. Something in her had just snapped. They were truthful reasons but I wanted to know why it happened just then, as it was completely out of character. This she couldn't answer at first, and we talked about other elements affecting our responses to things. Whether we are tired or frustrated, there are times when we feel out of control, and it is knowing this and being self-aware that is important. By the end of the conversation, she acknowledged she was feeling left out because Nadia had organised a playdate and not invited her. So, in fact, her reaction had been in anger to this, and we talked about how that felt and how it was normal to feel the emotion, but that there were ways to control it.'

Anger is a primary emotion that can be defused quickly. One of the techniques Leticia teaches her students is to breathe through it – slowly and deeply – before reacting to it. It is a way to calm the mind and be able to make better decisions. Teaching children self-regulation should be an integral part of their school day.

'Jessica needed my help to understand what the trigger to her behaviour had been. She couldn't do it alone. Frustratingly, her mum then came into the classroom later that day and tried to grab Nadia. My empathy with my students is limitless, but I have less patience when adults behave badly. I told her to get out of my classroom and we would talk elsewhere. Jessica moved schools a year later.'

Dealing with a parent's expectations and frustrations can be hard for a teacher to face. Leticia has a clear code of conduct, which she developed at the beginning of her career, based on her early experiences. Like the story of sweet Holly, a young Black student who had been adopted at the age of four by a wealthy white woman. Her mother had a retinue of staff to look after Holly and her sister, Beth. The girls were paraded around, dressed in nice clothes, with their hair straightened. Holly had almost everything but what she needed most were friends.

'I am a big advocate of young students playing and building relationships after school, not sitting down to do more schoolwork, so I didn't give homework. Holly was a good student. She didn't need to study more, she needed to have fun. It wasn't long before the principal called me into her office and I was faced with Holly's mother, who said, "Have you seen the colour of my children's skin? Do you think they are going to be anyone if they don't get into an Ivy League university? They need homework!" Then she told me how Beth was pretty and could be Oprah or Beyoncé but Holly wasn't, which meant homework was even more important to her. It was atrocious.'

Leticia took a deep breath and told the mother that she understood why she thought homework was important, but they were already covering everything they needed to in class. Instead, she said she thought it would be beneficial for Holly to connect with her roots.

'Holly had been openly talking about how she was similar to and different from the rest of the class and I thought she was asking great questions. I said she should be encouraged to discover more about her culture. Her mother was furious and yelled at me. I don't know what happened to Holly but I hope she found her answers.'

Her biggest advice to parents is to listen to their children with curiosity, without judgement, to ask more questions and turn that into self-reflection and shared exploration.

'As a society, we are taught to give answers and come up with conclusions and great ideas, but we aren't taught to ask questions. As parents, we are often guilty of discouraging or ignoring questions, but instead we should encourage children to ask more. If we don't all ask more questions we are going to be stuck with the same answers.'

Following five years in New York, Leticia and her family returned to Brazil and she began looking for teaching jobs. After years of study, several awards and vast work experience, she was told she didn't qualify to even be a teaching assistant. The Brazilian system was suspicious of her American education and commitment to social emotional learning (SEL). Instead, Leticia took matters into her own hands, including setting up a learning disabilities project and establishing a free SEL programme for public schools that is now accessed by two million students. These experiences led her to her entrepreneurship goal – to set up her own school along with three business partners. Camino in São Paulo transforms traditional teaching into active learning and champions three crucial principles – to take authorship of our lives, to be part of the bigger picture and to focus on the learning relationship between teacher, student and parent.

It is an amazing achievement and exactly what you would expect from the trailblazing Leticia. She believes every child has challenged her to be a better teacher and has played an integral part in the school she is so rightly proud of today. In education, we are constantly asking permission, but Leticia sees what needs to be done and gets on with it. She reacts to the culture, the needs of her students and the environment they are in, and vows to take every student on their own path.

'The turning point for me was many years ago when there was a terrible storm. The children were stuck at school while the storm raged around us. There was mess everywhere, pieces of roof falling and no electricity.'

The school told the students to stay in their classrooms and the teachers pretended they weren't in the middle of an extreme weather condition. At first Leticia reassured the frightened children but, as the worst of the storm passed, she felt she should empower her still-quivering students.

'I thought this is ridiculous, we can't ignore what is happening. I got them in three groups and gave one the task of getting cleaning materials; the second group took iPads out to interview people about the storm and the third group had big plastic bags to collect debris like leaves and branches. We spent all day immersing ourselves in the experience. The other teachers thought I was reckless but the community around these kids had been destroyed and they were supposed to sit and wait for someone to come in and clean up? They were ten years old and they had a chance to make a difference in that moment. There is no better learning experience.'

I love Leticia's attitude to her students. As teachers, we can be in control too much, and sometimes we need to let go. Give children responsibility and they thrive on it. Allow them to take the lead occasionally and they will rise to the challenge.

Armando Persico

55, Bergamo, Italy

'We should all have esteem for each other. Not just respect, that word doesn't seem enough. In Italy, esteem means a level above respect and that is what we should all exhibit. I think parents need to show this for their children because, in turn, this will teach children how to show it too'

Armando lives in the hills of Bergamo, in the Lombardy region of Italy. He loves being immersed in nature and now embraces life like never before, after a tough couple of years during COVID. His community was at the centre of the first outbreak and he said the sound of constant ambulance sirens drowned out the birdsong. Joy is returning to his family as he excitedly prepares to be a grandfather for the first time and takes a step back from his illustrious teaching career.

After studying economics at university, Armando had been a chartered accountant for ten years when he received a chance phone call from a local private school. They were looking for a teacher to lead their accountancy course for fourteen- to nineteen-year-olds and they asked him if he was interested. What felt like a welcome career diversion turned quickly into a passionate vocation when Armando realised this was exactly where he was supposed to be.

'I came face to face with humanity, it was amazing. I spent time with the students and I realised their reason to study didn't come from books, it came from life, so I changed my teaching approach and established an entrepreneur apprenticeship programme. I think we should begin with learning through experience before turning to books. If we start with a practical focus, it brings a subject alive for the students and then they respond to the written work much better.'

Like every exceptional teacher I have spoken to, Armando puts the student at the centre of the teaching and responds to what they need. His school operated in this way too, focusing more on student well-being than their grades, which is still an unusual approach. Armando believes that if teachers discuss why they are teaching then they will understand the importance of their role.

'The danger is to fall into an assembly line where we are turning out products, not people. Instead, we looked at each student and their different needs so we could work out their individual starting points and help them grow. I am lucky to work in a private system that allows us this luxury, but it should be standard for all schools.'

Twenty per cent of Armando's students have become entrepreneurs, which is significantly higher than the normal average of three per cent. Over 200 of them have gone on to create at least 2,000 jobs and valuable opportunities for the community.

'This is the best result and as their teacher, I feel a huge sense of personal achievement too. In the work I do with my students, teaching them how to establish their own businesses, I tell them if they take risks they must also take the responsibilities that come with this.'

It's a dynamic, brave approach and an extraordinary achievement. Armando has empowered his students to step into careers they have built themselves, to take a gamble and to give back. One of the ways he has done this is to put them into small, collaborative groups. Cooperative learning with your peers is a powerful tool and it teaches students to communicate with others as well as protecting their own voice. This is a life skill whatever path they take in the future.

'In a group, they must first have trust in each other. This is key. And they must respect the act of study and be curious about it, not defeated, bored or dismissive. I see positive behaviour in small group structures.'

As the teacher, Armando empowers the groups by stepping back but remaining present. It's a difficult balance to achieve but he wants them to be able to express themselves fully, without limitation.

'I tell them I know a lot of things and I am there to help them but they each have to become the protagonist in their own life. I can support them in their problem-solving but I am not going to do it for them. When I changed my way of teaching, I saw how much more confident students were when they were able to take responsibility for who they became.'

This is a good note for parents too. We are so conditioned to jump in and sort out our children's problems rather than give them the tools to deal with it themselves. There is a danger we are bringing up future adults who are unequipped to manage any issues they face. One of the students who benefited from this method was sixteen-year-old Roberto, who also had an additional issue to overcome. He had a debilitating stammer. When Armando first met him, it took Roberto several minutes to finish a sentence.

'You can imagine the idea of public speaking for him was very difficult. He was incredibly capable but his confidence was non-existent because of his stammer. We started a mini company with his group and then I looked at tackling the role he played within it.'

Armando met Roberto's parents. They had assumed his stammer would be with him throughout his life, but Armando had a plan. He asked them to meet him, with Roberto, once a month, to share the steps he was taking to deal with the problem and discuss their son's progress. Their involvement was key to Roberto being supported in every area of his life. Armando also decided to give him more responsibilities in the student group, and over the coming weeks his confidence grew.

'After only a few months, I could see Roberto's perception of himself was changing. As he worked to build the company, he realised what he was creating was his. It wasn't me telling him what to do and think, the solutions were his and his team's and so were the problems. He had ownership of something and deep pride in it.'

At the end of the term, the group had to present an elevator pitch. Roberto went to Armando and told him he thought he was ready to stand up in front of an audience and speak.

'He did it! There was a momentum to his presentation. He was talking about something he was passionate about and he spoke quickly but confidently. He did not stammer once. I think this is because he believed in himself.'

Roberto now owns an insurance company, with thirty employees, and Armando is, quite rightly, fiercely proud of him. And Roberto feels the same way towards his great teacher; they are still in touch now. It is the relationship between student and teacher that shines out to me here, how Armando gave Roberto the best environment for him to thrive in and included his parents in the journey. Armando is quick to point out he wasn't always able to provide this for his students.

'In the early days of teaching, I made mistakes. I learned more from those than I did my successes, and I still think about them today. Like one of my students, Simona.'

Simona had been struggling at school for a while. Tests were looming and Armando could see she was completely unprepared, with no concept of what she was doing. He thought it was impossible for her to continue, so he stopped her sitting the exam.

'I thought this was the best decision for her at the time. It wasn't, it was the wrong one. I still think she would have failed the exam but that isn't the point. I should have made the decision with the team of teachers I worked with. If I had seen her through other people's eyes they may have spotted something that I hadn't.'

Simona dropped out of school but, twenty-five years later, she is happily settled with a family of her own. But the memory still weighs heavy on Armando. He will always wonder if it was a missed opportunity for her. From a positive perspective, the situation turned into the catalyst he needed and it prompted him to become the teacher he is today.

'It taught me to believe in the students and respect the triangle of school, parent and pupil. We should all have esteem for each other. Not just respect, that word doesn't seem enough. In Italy, esteem means a level above respect and that is what we should all exhibit. I think parents need to show this for their children because, in turn, this will teach children how to show it too.'

Working with young people is incredibly rewarding but there are always individuals or stories that define the harder times and change you as a teacher. Armando is at the end of his career and is about to retire, so I am keen to know the one message he would share with the world.

'Keep being surprised. I saw that spark in Roberto's eyes when he realised he could do it. And this has been the most enjoyable part of what I do, seeing students surprise themselves. As children, we have this ability, but we begin to lose it as we grow up and when we become adults it is almost impossible to find. We should all have moments of surprise.'

What a wonderful outlook on life.

Mio Horio

37, Shiga Province, Japan

'Academic knowledge is important, but what's more, I want students to understand how that knowledge is connected with the real world. Then they will discover the real pleasure of learning'

Mio was born and brought up in a rural community in the Shiga province of Japan. While studying for her degree in English and speech communication, she visited Sri Lanka, where she saw and understood the difficulties facing an underdeveloped country and how education was the key to progression. She also volunteered in Vietnam at an international camp, teaching English to children in an orphanage. Mio didn't set out to become a teacher but, from that moment, it was clear to her where her destiny lay.

'Although the Vietnamese children didn't have parents, they lived as a family, so they were happy. Still, I knew education was very important for them and their only real chance to build an independent life with a good job and salary. It was then that I knew what I wanted to do.'

Thirteen years ago, Mio returned to Shiga province as an English teacher, an unpopular subject back then.

'We are surrounded by mountains that are said to be the tombs of the rulers from ancient times. Teaching English in such a community can be hard. When I started, most students were not interested in the language because they couldn't envisage using it. I had to fight to teach students who didn't like English or were taking it only because they needed it to enter university. Still, I found some students interested in foreign affairs and languages. I wanted to cherish their curiosity.'

Over nine years ago, Nana, a student in Mio's English class, told her that she wanted to take part in Japan's national Prefectural English Debate Tournament. Nana liked English better than other subjects, but she was nowhere near the level needed to take part in the competition. Mio told her she would need to encourage more of her fellow students if she wanted to participate, but didn't expect Nana to take it seriously.

'The next day she came with three more students who wanted to join the debate team. For a moment, I was at a loss. These were students who frequently frustrated teachers. In addition to being late for school and skipping classes, they didn't follow rules and ignored the teachers. I, along with my colleagues, was sure these children would drop out of the challenge.'

Intrigued, Mio was happy to help them for as long as they showed interest, so she invited two more students to complete the group and gained support from a colleague who was an expert in English debate. As the teachers expected, the students were overwhelmed. However, they did have good English pronunciation – gained from watching the Harry Potter films countless times – and Mio could see a glimmer of potential. The theme of the tournament was related to Japan's policy on trading, so they needed to research in Japanese first. This was complicated enough for the students, who were not used to academic study or learning about current affairs.

'It was hard to comprehend any of them rising to this challenge, let alone debating it in English. And yet, amazingly, they persevered. It was when they joined the practice match with another school that I noticed their progress. In the match, our team was defeated outright. My students couldn't answer any questions asked by the opposing team, couldn't comprehend what the opponents said, and they couldn't make any points by themselves.'

Throughout the rounds, they ended up repeating the statements and rebuttals that Mio and her colleague had put together. At moments, Mio had to step in, because some of the words were too hard for them and they had to repeat phrases and sentences after her. This doesn't sound like progress.

'This experience built a fire under them. The day after the debate was the weekend and they asked me if they could come to school to work on a practice match. I thought they would give up after their defeat but they showed true grit and resilience. They loved it!'

During the week, they would stay on after school to continue their research and preparation. Each weekend they returned to practise speaking and listening skills. Even when they were on an unrelated school trip, they would ask Mio questions and spent the evenings away practising with her. Mio was tired but she didn't want to let them down.

'We couldn't believe that the students who had often skipped classes were staying after school on weekends. As their effort bore fruit, their self-esteem and interest in the academic field increased. When the tournament was held, they were able to comprehend what their opponents said and could make rebuttals without the teachers' help.'

In a tournament of ten teams, held three months after that practice match, the team lost two matches, one ended in a draw and, finally, they won one. Although this meant the team could not place in the tournament, one of the students was awarded second prize in the Best Debater Award.

'The entire team cried for joy the moment their name was

announced, and my eyes were filled with tears. What made me most proud was how they gradually changed their mindset and showed perseverance to achieve their own goal. The time I spent with them created some of the best memories of my teaching career and it taught me how rewarding it is to work with young people.'

Mio believes her role was to bridge the gap between the students and their goal. She achieved this by closer communication, working on prep materials and carefully managing how much help she gave. Too much and the students wouldn't do anything for themselves, but just enough and it empowered them to reach their target. Ultimately, what they gained was something more precious than an exam score; it was incredible personal growth.

'And Nana taught me two things. Firstly, that curiosity really matters. She hated studying but enjoyed communicating, and her interest spurred her on to do some truly challenging work. The passion she showed made me believe in her too. And that was the second lesson, to have faith in a student's potential so you can help them realise it.'

Nana went on to major in English at a university of foreign studies and now works for an international airline, travelling the world.

Although Mio learned that teachers can empower students by staying closer to them, she was faced with another issue. About eight years ago, she returned to her old high school. Students there had much higher autonomy and English proficiency. However, their main motivation was to get better scores in exams, and they mainly studied to enter a university. Besides, they are not confident in themselves and hesitate to use English in communicating with people who have different cultural backgrounds.

'I wanted to have them practise English in a more authentic context, but we had few such opportunities. So, I started to use web-conferencing tools to connect students with those outside Japan. Then it brought some secondary effects, such as cultural and diversity understanding, and realising the potential of language learning.'

A few years ago, one of her pupils, Erika, was preparing for an English presentation. The topic was about the Muslim community, something she had no experience of or interaction with.

'Her presentation was full of stereotypes and prejudice. Her research had come from the internet and she didn't question the information. I contacted a Muslim friend, Madiha, and asked if my students could talk to her. Erika and her classmates then interviewed her and created a piece of work that represented a female Muslim viewpoint, something we don't always see reflected in Japanese media.'

It broadened Erika's horizons and positively shifted her original stance. Mio believes one of the biggest lessons her students learned from the experience was the importance of global communication and finding a shared language to use. I am passionate about this too.

'Their native language was Japanese, Madiha's was Urdu, but they communicated through the use of English. Without this ability, they wouldn't have been able to connect so easily. Of course, they can develop their language skills through some activities like English debates. However, it is not until the moment they actually practise it that they fully realise the potential of language learning. It is one of my biggest pleasures, as an English teacher, to see my students understand the potential of using language and break the barrier of stereotypes.'

Erika is now studying to be a teacher.

'I believe education should be sustainable and offered equally. At that time when I was teaching Nana and Erika, I was often frustrated at the gap between schools. Even though there were some students who were interested in learning about other cultures and foreign languages, we could not provide them with any authentic experiences due to several issues such as a short budget. On the other hand, some selected schools got enough financial support and implemented some programmes with foreign schools. This is unfair.'

Mio believes it is important to be closely connected to her students so that she can support them and help them when they consider their future. She thinks teachers need to have a better understanding of their students and that parents need to know their children deeply. She has students with an unwavering drive to succeed, which comes from their parents' expectations and hopes as well as from self-motivation. While this approach results in a ninety per cent university pass rate, it triggers concern.

'It is normal for students to finish school with us at 6 p.m. and then attend a "cram school" and continue to study until 10 p.m. before they finally go home. We get really worried about their health because they don't go to bed until about midnight so they are very tired, often suffering from headaches and falling asleep during classes in the day. I would rather help them to pursue their curiosity toward their interests than exam scores. Nana's change taught me that teachers' support can help to develop their perseverance and grit. Academic knowledge is important, but what's more, I want students to understand how that knowledge is connected with the real world. Then they will discover the real pleasure of learning.'

Mio wants parents to put their energy into learning who their children are, not what they should be learning.

Akash Patel

31, Dallas, USA

'I found a gap in global education in rural Oklahoma, I could have easily ignored it and assumed somebody else could take care of it. But when you see a gap in life, you fill it. You don't just stop there, you go find the next gap and then the next. You keep filling those gaps'

Akash Patel has the widest smile and the biggest heart and is one of the fastest speakers I have ever met. He was a finalist in the Global Teacher Award in 2018, the year I won, and we have been firm friends ever since. I was one of the evaluators for his application to the United States Citizenship and Immigration Services and was delighted and relieved that, after eleven years of dedication and commitment to education in America, he could finally call the country his permanent home. Unsurprisingly, he is incredibly passionate about immigration reform and the plight of immigrant children, which is reflected in his work as president elect of the American Council on the Teaching of Foreign Languages.

'I am the first Indian American to serve as president elect, and the youngest. I speak six languages, so I am thrilled to be the face of a country that is struggling to come to terms with a bilingual, multicultural society. You know, we could just coexist happily. It's great for our American children to be the global citizens of tomorrow and champions of anti-bigotry and anti-prejudice.'

Akash emigrated from India to the United States of America as a teenager with his twin brother, Happy. He says there can be a stereotype of 'brown Indians' being engineers, lawyers, doctors or a disgrace to the family. He plumped for nuclear engineering and was given a full-ride scholarship at Iowa State University, but at the end of his first semester he began to question the idea of spending thirty years of his life with nuclear reactors, rather than people.

He bought a second-hand SUV with Happy and they drove through the winter, from Iowa all the way down south to Oklahoma, where their uncle lived. Akash worked part-time jobs to put himself through a community college for teacher training. He was the only 'brown man' to graduate, along with students who were farmers, ranchers or family members from that community.

'They would invite me to rodeos and I would wear my cowboy hat and everyone assumed I was a Mexican cowboy as I spoke Spanish. When I told them I was from India they would say, "Bet you can see elephants on the streets there." And I would joke and tell them, yeah, sure you can. Just depends how much you have been drinking.'

We all have stereotypes, Akash believes. When he came to Oklahoma he expected to see cowboys and tepees.

'We may not look the same, we may not share the same fate. But you and me, Andria, can speak together and realise that we are both humans with shared passions, pursuits and dreams for our families, students and communities. Maybe we don't share a common language but we are connected through common humanity, which is what I found in Oklahoma.'

When Akash started teaching in small rural communities, people would stare at him in the street, but the children were inspired by his tales of travel – of working with elephants in India and sea turtles in Costa Rica and Sri Lanka. They wanted to hear more and he realised that, while a person can only physically be in one place, he had lots of friends across the world and if he could introduce them to his students, imagine the stories they would share? So many children do not have the privilege or resources to travel, so Akash decided to bridge the gap.

In 2014 he started video-calling his Facebook friends to ask them talk to the students in the classroom. He turned it into a game: the children had to ask questions to find out where the person was from. Fast-forward to 2021 and he now has 1,200 volunteers from over 150 countries who call classrooms in all fifty states in the United States, so that children from rural Alaska or San Juan, Puerto Rico, for example, can have access to somebody from pretty much anywhere in the world, from the UK and Germany, to India and Australia.

'The idea was simple. It was to promote global citizenship. My passion is to inspire global citizenship in youth.'

Now the non-profit organisation he leads connects over 1,000 language classrooms a month, reaching students learning Chinese, Japanese, German, French, Hindi or Swahili, to name just a few.

Akash has only been teaching for six years. He started in pre-service teaching, an internship, in small rural communities in Oklahoma before qualifying, and has continued to teach in low-socioeconomic status schools. He now teaches in an inner-city school in Texas where all the students are on one hundred per cent free or reduced lunches, so that gives some idea of the demographic. As a Spanish teacher, Akash connects his class with people from each of the twenty-one Spanish-speaking countries, including the tiny country Equatorial Guinea, a former Spanish colony in Africa.

'My kids are so incredible. They inspire me every single day.'

Like eighth-grader, Gonzalez. He was a difficult student to work with and extremely mischievous, so it was impossible to make him understand how important his learning was. Akash decided to video-call some students in Cuba.

'And they could only use internet for an hour with their internet card which cost $1, which is like twenty-two per cent of the $20 they make a month. When Gonzalez heard this, he instantly questioned why they didn't have WiFi or the internet. And how come they only made $20 a month.'

Gonzalez started researching more about Cuba and then Venezuela. He came across a story on CNN about people being so desperate for food because of the economic crisis, they were killing dogs in the street and eating them to avoid starving to death. This was transformative for Gonzalez. He told Akash he wanted to be a human rights lawyer.

'That's his ambition now. He says, "Mr Patel, I want to use my privilege in the United States to uplift the lives and voices of people in impoverished communities around the world." So that was also transformative for me because I'd had such a hard time dealing with this young man all year and suddenly, he has this remarkable empathy for homeless people.'

There are many stories Akash and I can share about students who have made as much of an impact on us as we have on them. Akash remembers connecting a group of his students with children from a tiny island in the Pacific Ocean who told them about how their homes were being flooded because of climate change. They talked about having to leave, and one of his class, Alexa, asked what a refugee was.

'She is a young lady born and brought up in Texas, and she had no idea what being a climate refugee meant. The next morning, she came into school with a picture she had drawn of her bed. She lives in a tiny one-bedroom apartment in inner-city Dallas. And she said,

"Mr Patel, I don't have money, but I think I could share my bed with one of the female students we met yesterday from the Kiribati Islands, because very soon their school is going to be underwater, and they're going to need a place to live."'

Akash is also driven by another motivation. Several years ago, in the middle of a test he was giving to his students, police officers turned up. His beloved twin brother, Happy, had been killed in a tragic accident. Akash was absent for three weeks and in that time his students, many from disadvantaged backgrounds, raised $3,000 to give to his family for the funeral. Akash tried to return the money but the students refused to take it back, so instead they turned it into a Happy Meals programme for the homeless. Since 2018 they have donated over 20,000 Happy Meals through a foundation Akash has set up in his brother's memory, the Happy World Foundation.

'Because we all deserve global experiences and through these global experiences, it leads to a Happy Planet free of prejudice and bigotry. That's my vision. That's my life's calling. That was really inspired through my classroom teaching and the students' commitment to the cause.'

For all the wonderful moments, there are the truly agonising and vulnerable ones. Like the time Akash was accused of teaching terrorism by a parent who was not happy about him sharing a story about the Pakistani activist, Malala Yousafzai. They thought he was teaching them about Islam. To this day he is not sure how this got so confused. He did discuss it with the father, and ended up having one of the greatest relationships he's ever had with a parent.

'It made me realise what kind of a place I was teaching in. That it was so small that anything different from their culture could raise an eyebrow.'

We have to address tough subjects and answer questions in the classroom in a neutral way, but we are not there when the students recount those stories back at home. Luckily, the principal of the school knew and trusted Akash.

'I said, here's the lesson. Here's the news article that we read about how these young ladies were so brave, that despite what they were facing, in that community, they were courageous enough to walk to school every day, even though terrorists were after them. And that's why they shot them, because they didn't want any female going to school. It was a tough conversation. The only reason faith was brought up was because the kids asked me why she had a head-covering on. And that's when you should address these questions. I realised that was a really beautiful chance for me to turn this into an opportunity for teaching cross-cultural understanding.'

When I ask Akash what makes a great teacher, he says it starts with names. He has 200 students learning Spanish this year and he knows everyone's name. It means so much to them, that he knows they exist and remembers things, like an ability they may have, or a situation they have been in. He also connects with parents.

'I think parents are shifting that focus in a lot of our communities where it's like, hey, it's the teacher's job, the teacher's responsible for my child. But it's even more impactful when the parent is directly involved. I don't blame the parents, they are working, single parents, some kids have parents who are incarcerated. The children live with their grandparents or in foster care. But just reading to their child for ten minutes before bed . . .'

Akash has a student whose father was sadly deported back to Aguascalientes in Mexico, so they video-call him and he joins the class and teaches them more about where he is from. It brings him into his daughter's school day and makes her feel that he is part of it.

'If we can get families involved, we can show the kids that we care about their backgrounds, how we value them as humans, we know their likes and dislikes. We know what makes them happy. We know what they're passionate about. We help ignite their superpowers in our classrooms. And if we can get the parents involved, man, we can work some magic.'

I have met so many great teachers who still don't have what Akash possesses. It's the X factor, the special quality that turns him from good into magnificent. He cites his college professor, Dr Jeanne Ramirez Mather, as one of his biggest influences, saying he would go to her classes because she would always talk about something multicultural. She created a programme over twenty-five years ago, donating books to desperately poor children in inner cities and rural communities of Oklahoma, and to date she has given over 250,000 new books.

'She was so resourceful and I feel like she inspired the entrepreneurial spirit in me, the social entrepreneur that I am today with the non-profit I created and run in my brother's memory and the non-profit that I'll now lead on a national level.'

Dr Ramirez also ran a toy driver, a charity fundraiser in aid of Syrian child refugees. Amazingly, the predominantly farming, rancher community and pre-service teachers got together 2,300 toys. And two of those farmer colleagues of mine drove their car from Oklahoma to Washington DC, to the Institute of Peace, so that they could ship them to refugee Syrian children in camps around the globe.

So, I ask Akash, if you could share one piece of advice what would it be?

'You know, for me, it would be to find the gaps in life. I found a gap in global education in rural Oklahoma, I could have easily ignored it and assumed somebody else could take care of it. But when you see a gap in life, you fill it. You don't just stop there, you go find the next gap and then the next. You keep filling those gaps.'

Daisy Mertens

34, Venray, The Netherlands

*'Sometimes the power is not to know the answers.
As a teacher you have moments during the
day where you don't know the answer but it's
what you do with the question. Speak to the
child, ask a colleague, go online, read a book'*

From a young age, Daisy escaped difficulties in her home life by going to school. As she cycled there each morning she would feel her mood change, knowing she was going to be in a safer environment. After fourteen years working in education, she can now see this was the catalyst to her becoming a teacher.

'For me, school was associated with finding freedom without worry. I could play, learn and forget about all the unpleasantness at home. It enabled me to turn my past into something beautiful and positive. It was one of my life lessons.'

At teacher training college, Daisy admits, she was far from the ideal student and didn't take studying seriously. After her second year, she was close to being failed until a lecturer confronted her and asked her what her most important values in teaching were. This one conversation was a turning point for Daisy as it changed her perception of what kind of student she wanted to be in teacher training. From that point, she concentrated on her studies and felt an intrinsic motivation.

'Within a few hours, I was able to answer the question, and the answer is just the same today. My values are reflection, autonomy, self-confidence, self-efficacy and, most importantly, my relationship with my students.'

In her third year of training, Daisy was placed in the multicultural school in her hometown for her internship.

'I cried on my first day because I was overwhelmed, it was very different from the school I had attended as a child. I was not used to the wonder of a multicultural environment and there was a stigma around this type of school. As a child, I attended a predominantly white, Christian school, although I was very different from my friends because my mother is half-Indonesian and a cleaner. Then, as a child, I was the odd one out.'

After her first day at the school, Daisy was excited because she knew this was where she was meant to be.

'I felt I could add something to these children's lives. They needed knowledge but they also needed to feel safe and loved, and I recognised that.'

When Daisy qualified, she chose not to work in her hometown, instead taking on the challenge of a city primary school situated in a deprived area. She is still there today, one of forty-five staff, teaching 415 students from over thirty nationalities. Daisy teaches children aged ten to twelve who have challenges with language and maths. She leads a theme-based learning approach full of knowledge, language and reading as well as coordination of the educational quality in her school. In 2016, she was awarded National Teacher of the Year in Primary Education.

'Who would have thought that someone from a small village in the south of the Netherlands, raised in a single-parent family and troubled circumstances, could receive such recognition?'

Winning a prestigious award is not Daisy's greatest accomplishment. For her, the biggest achievements come through the process of teaching. It is about the whole experience. She doesn't rest on her laurels but continues to grow, reading and researching to better herself and make a bigger impact on her profession.

'I want to keep developing myself. It's a never-ending story.'

Daisy has many stories of amazing students but she will never forget one girl, and the class she was part of. Lila was seven years old and had been diagnosed with a brain tumour. She was in Daisy's class until she was too poorly to return to school after the summer holiday. Lila's parents invited Daisy over to visit at the weekend, and Daisy read *Cinderella* to her. Daisy could see that Lila was nearing the end of her life. After she had finished reading Daisy joined the sick girl's parents in the garden for a chat.

'Her mother went to check on her daughter and came running out screaming for help. Lila was struggling to breathe. Her mother and I tried to resuscitate her but I knew there was nothing we could do. It was so hard but I had to say to the mother that we needed to stop. At that moment, I took charge because, although Lila's parents and grandmother were there, it was absolute chaos. Awful for them all.'

The doctor was called, even though it was too late, and Daisy waited with them. When she left, she contacted the teaching staff and they gathered together to discuss how they would deliver the news to Lila's classmates on Monday. They had guidance and counselling from a grief support group and Daisy prepared to face the children. Several students had been to Lila's house to keep her company, so Daisy knew how upset they would be.

'I spent the weekend trying to work out how I would tell the children that she'd died, and on Monday morning I went into the classroom with some of my colleagues. I decided to just go with my intuition and stop overthinking it. It was the most beautiful conversation I have ever had with young children. Of course, there was much sadness, but also an acceptance that Lila was no longer ill and was going to heaven. One child said his goldfish had died recently and he hoped Lila and the fish would be together.'

In this moment, Daisy saw how pure and uncomplicated children are and the way they view things. They always look for the positivity and hope in a situation. She had approached the issue with a grown-up rationale rather than through a child's perspective.

'As adults, we should try to look at things through the eyes of a child sometimes. It helps me relate to things, not just in my work as a teacher but in my life too. This was the lesson I learned from Lila and her amazing classmates.'

Before the pandemic, Daisy was working with Her Royal Highness Princess Laurentien of the Netherlands, on a project focused on child participation. In one of the sessions, the princess interviewed children about what they thought teachers could do better and how they rated the Dutch education system. The children were very honest.

'We took it all in. Adults accept direction and criticism more when it comes from children. Between adults there are biases and misconceptions, but children just say what they think, and this allows us to be more open too.'

Daisy always asks her students for feedback and uses it to improves her lessons. While it can be hard for adults to accept feedback from a colleague, many acknowledge it better when it is from a child, and find ways to do something about it. Daisy strongly advocates the importance of including the students' voice and their input in school development across the education system.

There have been countless challenges in her career, but Daisy embraces them with the vigour and commitment you would expect from someone who is no stranger to them. Her motto is that every child gets a new chance after every break. Everything resets and they start again. One of Daisy's recent students pushed the behavioural boundaries constantly.

'Arnando was severely dyslexic and had a difficult home situation where neither of his parents were educated, so there was no encouragement. I had to find ways to establish a good relationship with him and motivate him because he did not read or write. I was regularly setting him new goals to reach every day, like making eye contact, reading a few pages of his book and writing some notes. It was slow progress, but it worked.'

Daisy believes she is the owner of her learning process, but the co-owner, along with the students, of their learning process. She is the leader in the classroom and asks questions of the children, but she wants to enable her students to question her too.

'Sometimes the power is not to know the answers. As a teacher you have moments during the day where you don't know the answer but it's what you do with the question. Speak to the child, ask a colleague, go online, read a book.'

Parents play a big part in the education ecosystem. School is not the only place where the learning happens, but Daisy worries about those parents who have so little hope for themselves that they cannot convey it to their children. How can you reflect it if you don't feel it yourself? And how do your own feelings reflect on your child?

'There was a father who was furious because his daughter had low grades. He could not understand how she had not done better. I told him his child was a role model for every other pupil in the classroom, she worked hard and this was where her ability was. It wasn't about motivation and he had to change his response to acknowledge the positives and not crush her with his disappointment. Parents need to think about what their children will take away from their reactions.'

It's about expectations – whether they are high, unrealistic or non-existent – and how a parent communicates this to their child. Parents often teeter between how much praise they can give compared to how far they can continue to push for better achievements. It is treading a fine line. Daisy thinks parents shouldn't share crushing disappointment, and that they should trust the school to tell them what their child is capable of.

Recently, Daisy has been made a member of the National Education Council in the Netherlands – only the second teacher on the council in the last hundred years. It's a huge honour, but it is also an opportunity for her to see what the ministry is doing and how the educational councils and organisations work. As importantly, there should be a teacher at this table.

'I was worried that I may be underqualified for the position, but I reflect the confidence I want my students to show, and I will carry on.'

The addition of her voice is vital because so often the people who make decisions about education are not working in it. There should be a 'Daisy' leading the education system in every country.

Manuel Calcagni

35, Santiago, Chile

'We can talk about a good movie for hours and I hear different opinions and visions of the world. I learn a lot from my students through these conversations and in the short films they make. They have helped me understand the world better. I am always learning from the differences'

Manuel has spent the last nine years teaching in the oldest high school in Chile. Situated in the capital, Santiago, the public boys' school welcomes students from every corner of the city, so there is a diverse mix of cultures and backgrounds. There are around 4,400 students studying at the school, with an oversubscribed forty-five of them to a class. While the school has a long tradition of excellence, this has been harder to maintain in recent years, partly due to a lack of resources. Manuel has witnessed a difficult time for education in Chile.

'Students and teachers have been campaigning for better school conditions and for more money to be invested in their education. There have been a lot of protests at schools across the city, which have turned ugly.'

The violence has been shocking. Police have used tear gas and water cannons to break up the protests and many people have been arrested. While students are labelled as 'terrorists' and 'delinquents' for their behaviour in raising these issues, they often feel they have little choice.

'I understand how hard it is for them and how important it is to be heard, but they fight a lot. This is also not the answer. We need to find different ways to communicate that don't antagonise the police because it's dangerous and destructive. We are all tired, the school is old and it takes the focus away from the classroom.'

Manuel comes from a long line of teachers, including his grandparents and mother, who inspired him every day. His mother always shared ideas with him and he saw the impact her work made on her students. He followed in his grandfather's footsteps and became a history teacher.

'I also teach film studies, and focus on teaching key moments in history through movies. We watch many different films from around the world as well as making our own too. I established an after-school film club to involve the students in all areas of the movie-making process, from script, camerawork and recording to editing and film festivals. Teaching in this way gives students space to express themselves. They are very creative.'

I can see how powerful Manuel's approach is. It brings the students together over a common interest.

'We can talk about a good movie for hours and I hear different opinions and visions of the world. I learn a lot from my students through these conversations and in the short films they make. They have helped me understand the world better. I am always learning from the differences.'

For many, not only watching and discussing films but creating their own is a more productive way to learn than sitting in a classroom with a textbook. It's such a clever opportunity to connect and inform, because every child loves watching movies, and they gain and share such mixed perspectives. Manuel is not just referring to modern films like superhero franchises, although they have their place.

'It takes some work before students can understand context, but when they are ready I always show the same movie. It is a classic 1969 Chilean film called *El Chacal de Nahueltoro,* based on a true story about a farmer, who suffers years of abuse as a child, and becomes an alcoholic and a criminal. In the face of kindness shown to him by a woman and her children, he commits a heinous act and kills them when he is drunk. It's a brutal story but it's also one of the deepest ways to understand crime and how society and our past influences us.'

In analysing the film with his students, Manuel gains their insight and reflections from their unique standpoints. Not only does this story teach them about Chilean history, but it considers the very human theme of why people sometimes act as they do. It develops his students' critical thinking like it did for sixteen-year-old Dante, whose response to the film was life-changing.

'I will never forget his reaction. It's not an easy movie or topic to understand, but Dante put this old black and white movie into the context of the present day and his own experiences. He totally got it. Some of his friends had been arrested by the police during the protests and this film made him think of those boys, who were treated like criminals. We talked about why they were so angry, what made them act the way they did and how authority responded to them.'

It was an incredibly proud moment for Manuel. Dante is now studying public administration at university and they have kept in touch. He continues to watch films with an analytical eye and they still talk about the movie and quote lines to each other. Manuel is hopeful that Dante will find positive ways to channel his rebellion.

'The situation in Chile is changing, but it is far from resolved. In the midst of important political progress there are still protests and police intervention. I talk about it with my students and the movies we create sometimes work in sharing opinions if there is a disagreement. It is a better way to speak out than with petrol bombs.'

Film-making can also be used for much more personal stories. Manuel had a transsexual student, Domi, who was having a hard time being bullied at school, not just by students but by some teachers too. There were constant cruel remarks and anonymous notes, and she was not allowed to wear dresses. At home, her mother refused to accept her decision and continued to call her Pablo and use male pronouns. She assumed it was something she had done wrong in her parenting, unable to understand her child's decision.

The school had been exclusively for boys for over two hundred years but recently made the decision to welcome girls too. Manuel and his students made a short promotional film encouraging female students to come to the school.

'As part of the film, we interviewed and filmed Domi talking about her experience. She was honest about how tough it had been, but she said she was proud of herself because she felt she had made things easier for other transsexual students. I learned a lot from her, as did her classmates.'

The biggest lesson Manuel learned from Domi was about being brave. He watched her fighting every day, trying again and again to live her life the way she wanted to, whether this was to wear a dress instead of trousers, talk to a classmate about her feelings or cope with her mother's dismay. At the age of eighteen, Domi began hormone treatment, and is now studying music.

'I know how devastated Domi's mother was to begin with, but it wasn't about her life. It was about her child's future. Every one of my students is an individual and as they develop their knowledge and ability they may become people their parents didn't expect to meet. My job is to create democratic classrooms where a student can become themselves, and then they begin to teach us – the teachers and the parents. So, we must listen to them.'

Domi was incredibly brave, at home and at school. Don't forget, she was in an all-boys' school too.

'We had support from a psychologist and I spoke to her classmates and her mother regularly. I encouraged Domi to keep talking to them too. I found it a beautiful experience, to be by her side as she navigated through the complexities of her experience. As a teacher, I think it's important to make everyone feel good in the classroom, and that is the environment I try to create. We deal with problems, of whatever size.'

Manuel believes one of the best ways for parents to connect with their children is to watch films together too, and discuss them afterwards. It can be a starting point from which to talk about anything, and helps to shrink the generational gap. He has witnessed the power of this time and again.

'Sharing your favourite film with your children creates an intimate, joyful connection. I have a daughter now and I can't wait to watch movies with her. My favourite? I couldn't tell you. It changes all the time!'

Yasodai Selvakumaran

34, Sydney, Australia

'The truth is that teenagers should not be underestimated. And they often are. So, when people question why I choose to work with teenagers I say honestly, it's the best part of the job. It's the energy, the optimism, the idea that they can do anything and, as much as it's a really difficult time for a lot of students, it is about finding out who they are'

Fair equality of opportunity is a theme that Yasodai comes back to again and again when she talks about teaching. As a Sri Lankan-born Tamil, Yasodai understands the need for it perhaps more than many. Her family left Sri Lanka during the country's unrest and settled in rural Australia, where there was a distinct lack of diversity. As a teenager Yasodai hated being different.

'I just wanted to be like everybody else. I think that's a classic teenage response. And I was always uncomfortable sharing my own cultural background. I thought in Tamil, my first language, so that would sometimes create a strange syntax when I spoke.'

Several other formative experiences fuelled her growing passion to support cultural diversity. When she was at university in Sydney, she volunteered on an Aboriginal programme, the Australian Indigenous Mentoring Experience, which opened her eyes to issues facing Aboriginal and Torres Strait Islander students and communities in the inner-city area of metropolitan Sydney. From there she volunteered at a city school in Sydney, which taught her about inequality first-hand. She also took a part-time job at the YWCA, a women's organisation, helping students realise their full potential with a programme called Links to Learning.

'I was working with nine girls, at three different high schools, each one at risk of dropping out. So even before I went into my first teaching placement, I knew about how marginalised teenagers can feel, and how that can have an impact on a person's education.'

They were instrumental in cementing Yasodai's career choice, but also her philosophy of giving every student the opportunity to succeed no matter where they come from.

After graduating, Yasodai took a job in a school in a lower-socioeconomic area in western Sydney. The minute she first stepped through its doors as a trainee teacher, she immediately felt she was in the right place – she loved the welcoming atmosphere, the pupils' art on the walls and the strong mentorship from her peers. It's exactly how I feel about the school I teach in.

'There was a big focus on professional learning, a team approach that we are all in this together to improve the outcomes for our students. So when a placement came up I thought, this is where I want to be, even though my university colleagues suggested applying for other places. People thought it would be really hard there because it was an inner-city school with diversity problems – it had around forty different ethnicities.'

Despite her volunteer work, she wasn't prepared for how to deal with the differences in student ability, from those struggling with low literacy levels with English as their second language, to the gifted students who were sailing through exams. There was a huge range in each classroom and as a humanities and English teacher Yasodai felt it keenly. This was an ongoing focus of her own professional learning as part of the priorities of the school and the wider system. Yasodai then became a mentor herself and worked as part of a team supporting new teachers on lesson and learning design to target these student areas of need.

Student wellbeing can be a complicated issue for a teacher to deal with. A mental health first aid course also proved invaluable in giving her the confidence to cope with difficult situations, particularly when faced with some of her more underprivileged students and their tough backgrounds.

'I have students who are not living with their parents and I am always conscious that their home life is not the same as many of their peers. The same for those who are split between two parents or are in a single-parent family. I grew up in a very steady family home so other people's lives were a big eye-opener for me, just understanding what some of my students go through.'

Many of the students work part-time, some thirty hours a week outside of their schooling, and juggle learning with adult-type responsibilities.

'It's amazing what young people can cope with and still excel at. As much as I have seen them faced with serious challenges, I have also seen some prove how resilient they are, which has totally inspired me.'

Paradoxically, one of Yasodai's earliest teaching challenges came from a student, Eloise, who was very academic and gifted. Yasodai was teaching a compulsory history unit about the World Wars and Eloise said she didn't want to do it.

'She said why should I care? This is not my history. And I remember looking at her and thinking, I totally understand where you are coming from. And what you've just said can apply to so many people in this room. For me, that was a turning point.'

Eloise questioned the compulsory history courses in a way Yasodai never had, even though she too came from a different background and had not had the chance to explore her own heritage. The realisation shifted her thinking. Not only was there a fundamental discussion to be had about ignoring people's histories, but she also realised that if she couldn't engage one student who was happy at school and was good at it, then how was she going to catch the attention of those who struggled? And how could she give students an opportunity to share their own stories, find out more about their histories and understand how they belonged in multicultural Australia?

'I gave Eloise a chance to explain how she felt. I said I understood and asked what would she like to learn about if she could. She came from a country at war but she didn't know much about the issues and they weren't in the Australian textbooks. I told her my family also fled a war in Sri Lanka and that was the history of my background, which I also didn't know much about because I'd never been taught it, *and* I am a history teacher! I think that helped; there was a moment of connection between us where she saw that I empathised.'

Yasodai began to look for opportunities to address the issue and give students the chance to study what was more relevant to them alongside the standard curriculum. In addition, she taught elective history, which gave her more freedom in the subject, and Eloise not only chose to sign up but loved it. Yasodai designed an assessment task, asking students to create an exhibit for a public history exam to say why the story they had chosen was important and how they would represent it.

'I wanted to show students that history – their history – is an actual living, breathing thing. It's so important. Look at what we are living through now with COVID and how this will be remembered in the future globally.'

Yasodai also designed an assessment where they looked at terrorism and foreign policy and had to write a response as if they were advising the government. In doing so, they had to investigate historical approaches to this and how these could inform future responses.

'We had students who really struggled with their writing, but by the end of the two-year course every single child had written, rewritten and edited their work to an incredible standard. Not because we as teachers told them to, but because they took pride in what they were studying, and developed high expectations of themselves and their professionalism.'

I hugely admire the way Yasodai took on the challenge and found a creative, disciplined and vital answer to it. She knows there are many parents whose history is not being represented in their children's curriculum and she is keen to offer advice.

'Students need to be encouraged to discover transnational case studies with the help of their teachers, which they can then explore in broader project opportunities. And a brilliant way of bringing this history alive is for schools to link to cultural and public events that the family takes part in, and share and celebrate this within the school community.'

Yasodai talks about keeping an open heart and mind when it comes to teenagers, and to welcome learning in both formal and informal ways. With Eloise, it was about finding what grabbed her emotionally. Understandably, Yasodai is a big hit with her students. When she took parental leave they said one of the things they would miss about her was her laugh. They also recognised how she makes time for them to speak out and encourages them to give her feedback on her teaching too.

'It's important to surround ourselves with people who not only share our values but challenge us. Above all, I thrive on teaching my students how to have a respectful debate and compassion.'

Yasodai is one of the youngest teachers I am interviewing for this book, and yet her wisdom and experience shine out far beyond her years.

'The truth is that teenagers should not be underestimated. And they often are. So, when people question why I choose to work with teenagers I say honestly, it's the best part of the job. It's the energy, the optimism, the idea that they can do anything and, as much as it's a really difficult time for a lot of students, it is about finding out who they are. And I get to be part of that. So schools, society and parents, we must all give teens a voice at the table!'

Yasodai says in Australia now there has been a welcome shift in focus, with a student panel or presentation at many national curriculum conferences. It is important to give our young people a platform to tell their stories.

Her focus has always been on the student voice and making sure the issues they raise are valued and acted on, and she thrives on this.

'I've had some incredibly difficult personal issues that have come up for me. But I always wanted to be at work. Even when not coping at times myself personally, I walk into school and as I head to my classroom everyone says, "Good morning." And in that instant I know I want to be here. Regardless of the difficult things I may be juggling in my personal life at that moment.'

This is my experience of teaching too. Sometimes one of the best things about being in school is that for the time I am there the world outside doesn't exist. It's about my students and the work I can get done.

Yasodai is a problem-solver, a communicator and a listener who values the role she plays in her students' lives.

'Helping pupils find their strengths is a shared endeavour between them, the school and their families. One of the most rewarding elements of being a teacher is the impact I might have on the parents and the conversations I am part of. It is not just about what success looks like to the student but, often, what it looks like to their parents, and how we can align these if they differ. We need to make sure every voice is heard, most importantly the students'.'

Jiang Xueqin

46, Beijing, China

'It is what makes creativity possible, when different people with mixed skill sets come together. We would get successful, creative people and entrepreneurs, but also properly developed human beings'

Jiang was born in China, and moved to Canada when he was six. Chinese immigrants from a small rural village, Jiang and his family experienced a language barrier, economic difficulties and cultural issues, as they settled in the wealthy metropolis of Toronto. School was incredibly hard for Jiang, a distracted pupil who struggled academically, until he met one teacher who believed in him. She gave him books to read. She encouraged him and she awakened his intellectual interest. He found the school library and never left it.

Through his hard work and perseverance, Jiang won a full scholarship to Yale University, majoring in English literature. He credits this achievement to those teachers who saw his potential and supported him. He had similar encouragement from his professors at Yale, but the university experience was traumatic.

'I came from the opposite background to the other kids, who were hugely privileged. I didn't have any friends because we had different interests and values, and I did not know how to communicate with them. It was my first time away from home, which also triggered a deep yearning to discover my roots.'

When he graduated, Jiang wanted to contribute to the development of education; he knew that, done rightly, it had the potential to change lives. At the same time, he was curious about China, so he decided to return to his birthplace and teach English there. That was when he knew teaching was his destiny.

'I think teaching for me is intellectually stimulating – the idea that you take information and communicate it effectively so it inspires students to think deeply about life. My grandfather and father had been teachers in China, and I always paid attention to how my teachers taught me.'

Jiang is based in Beijing and has been teaching in China for twenty-five years. As well as now being a principal, he is heavily involved in education research, in which he can draw on his many and varied experiences. Jiang advocates helping people grow by creating a community of people who can support each other in this. He makes a fascinating and revolutionary comparison.

'You know, schools are not built for the education of children, they are built for the convenience of adults. I want schools to operate more like hospitals, in that you get individualised attention and feedback. Like doctors with their patients, teachers need to be aware of the emotional needs and learning trajectory of each individual student, so personal strategies can be devised.'

I think Jiang is one of the best types of maverick, who balances refreshing insights with realistic and considered thoughts and actions. While he questions the curriculum, he understands the need for structure. He just doesn't want it to limit the teacher's ability to think for themselves.

'I think we should be able to exercise our own judgement and discretion with our students. I think human beings are capable of that because we are all hard-wired to be teachers, right? To be caretakers of the younger generations and empower them to make their own choices.'

Literature is one of Jiang's big passions and he teaches the art of reading, among other subjects. He is selective about the texts he chooses because he wants them to resonate with his class. With each book, he invites his students to step fully into its world, and together they explore the story, characters and themes, taking an inquiry-based approach that enables them to become more observant, independent and sensitive to the world around them.

'My greatest achievement as a teacher is to inspire kids to want to read. I think that's the most important thing you can do. Chinese children often have a very narrow perspective of what learning is and focus on improving test scores. Demonstrating an advanced vocabulary is done by memorising word lists, but I convinced my pupils to read books. Only then can they have a true understanding of what the words mean. And the books act as portals for them to access other lives and worlds.'

Jiang encourages everyone to read together in class and helps them gain a set of skills to enable them to be critical readers. He likens his role to scaffolding, put in place while students build their competence and gain confidence. Once they see reading as a source of empowerment and liberation, he knows he has succeeded.

When Jiang became principal at his current school, he was told about fourteen-year-old Vincent, who had been labelled 'a problem child'. Vincent was overlooked at home and was a loner at school. He was a curious but introspective boy who spent his breaks wandering around the campus identifying vegetation.

'He had an encyclopaedic knowledge of plants and trees. In China, it's seen as strange for a child to be off doing his own thing. The teachers and other classmates thought he was weird. For a long time, he couldn't find his place at home or school, so he escaped into nature.'

The bigger concern was his insistence in bringing knives and blocks of wood to school. The teaching staff were perplexed and wanted Jiang to confront him and deal with the issue.

'I sat down and talked to him. I asked him why he brought knives and wood into school and he said he liked carpentry, that was his interest. I knew nothing about carpentry, so I asked him to tell me more about what he made and he was full of fascinating information. I suggested he give a presentation to his class, but he said he was too shy.'

Jiang gave Vincent the opportunity to talk about his passion. He explained to Vincent that the worry around him bringing knives in was not that he was mistrusted, but that another child could hurt themselves. In showing faith in Vincent, Jiang unlocked something.

'I asked Vincent if he could run a woodwork club after school, and again he said he was too shy. But over the weeks that followed I saw certain changes in him. He became a confident young man who was talking to his classmates more. He held his head high and his posture changed.'

One simple conversation made a big difference to Vincent. He began to see himself in a new light, and it inspired him to be more open, engaged and trusting in the people around him. Jiang understood him. This was the most powerful gift he could have given to Vincent. A few weeks later they talked again about the idea of a carpentry club, and Vincent said he would consider it. But then the pandemic hit.

'Like Vincent, each child is born to be his or her own person and we need to accept that. We forget that a child is a human being, worthy of respect and trust, and should be able to see the world in their own way. I have witnessed many parents being unhappy because their children become people they did not imagine them to be. But the child was never that person in the first place. You know the saying "Every child is a blank slate"? Well, that's not true. Every child is a soul with a distinctive personality.'

I think this is a powerful message for parents to hear, and something I will continue to reflect on.

Jiang didn't always see education this way. Early in his career he ran an elitist school programme that recruited the top students for a rigorous, academically stimulating experience. One year there were problems with recruitment and Jiang had a student group of mixed ability. The results surprised him.

'The less able students exceeded my expectations. In fact, they thrived in the programme because it offered a different way of learning and they responded to that. Many kids struggle to navigate the rigid Chinese school system but, in the environment I created, they were transformed, and they taught me not to discriminate in favour of the top students. The kids who find study hard are often much more open-minded, tolerant and willing to see their own faults. In life, they can do better than those who are traditionally academic.'

I think this is a fascinating observation, and it is something I have witnessed in my own career as a teacher. There have been countless examples of this throughout Jiang's teaching career, but one child stands out for him. William was a very nice boy, but a poor student who did badly in the high school examination. He was often the first one to raise his hand in class to answer a question but didn't always get it right, so his classmates constantly made fun of him. Despite his difficulties and the bullying he encountered, he never took it personally and continued to maintain a positive attitude.

'In the last year of high school the students have the opportunity to apply to a liberal arts college in the USA. The selection process involves an interview, rather than an examination. To my surprise, William got in. I was concerned because I knew he lacked the intellectual capacity to cope with it, but off he went. And the teachers adored him! He was always willing to ask questions, recognise his own failings and work hard.'

The college recommended he transfer to Columbia University for his third year. He applied and was accepted. When he graduated, he stayed in New York and is now a successful software engineer.

'He is still in touch with me. And just as inquisitive for life and full of gratitude for his education. He's a great human being. And sometimes schools don't care about great human beings, we care about great students. And there's a difference.'

Jiang pinpoints a big issue with those Chinese students who are singled out as geniuses and focus on a very narrow set of abilities but cannot function in the real world. Many go to the most revered universities in the world like Oxford, Cambridge, Harvard and Yale, Jiang's alma mater, but once they get there they cannot handle the evaluation criteria.

'It's much more holistic than they are used to. The level of discussion is open-ended and abstract, and they are only used to a right or wrong answer. They have been schooled to do quick calculations and have a good memory, but they have not been taught how to be curious. So often they mentally break down, become depressed and envious of fellow students.'

Having a one-size-fits-all approach is a dangerous side effect of the education system and a worldwide problem. If a student struggles in maths then the answer seems to be to make them do more of it. There has to be another way to solve this.

'I say it's like having a broken foot and we should diagnose it properly and find ways to make it heal but instead we say, "Run more laps." That is what it feels like to be a student struggling at school, they just get given more homework to compensate. It's completely wrong.'

What Jiang teaches goes against the current of Chinese culture, society and an obsession with money. He encourages his students to be themselves, intellectually enquiring, less materialistic and interested in a lifetime of exploring ideas. Over the months, he sees his class shift their perspective and their individuality blossom. But he cannot change the culture on his own.

'They become infected by my sort of thinking. But then each child enters society and the pressure to make money and conform to society's narrow idea of success begins to take shape. They do what they are told, and some end up living a miserable and confusing life.'

I am keen to know what one thing Jiang would do if he could wave a magic wand over the education system that would benefit the children.

'It would be to promote collaboration. To show that it isn't just about individual achievements, but the ability to work and connect with others. It is what makes creativity possible, when different people with mixed skill sets come together. We would get successful, creative people and entrepreneurs, but also properly developed human beings.'

Jiang's mission is to reimagine how education could be and build a new school system. I have every faith in him.

Candida Couto

55, Porto, Portugal

'You know, the one truth I have discovered about children? They need attention. I tell parents, it takes five minutes, just ask your kids what they did and listen to the answer. And show them affection too'

In the first class Candida ever taught, she used an extract from a Portuguese poet and teacher, Sebastião da Gama, to introduce herself to the students. The quote was about the true essence of being a good teacher, which focused on wanting the children to be happy. That day she found her calling as a teacher, a profession that she continues to thrive in and which inspires her, thirty-six years later. Candida's motto now, as then, is for her students to be happy.

'I would say I am very lucky, I adore what I do and I constantly convey this message to my students. I am a very fulfilled teacher and so privileged to be in this position.'

For Candida, professional happiness has been hard-won. During her marriage, her job took a back seat to enable her husband's career to develop, and she focused on bringing up their two children. Following an acrimonious divorce some years later, Candida stepped back into full-time teaching. She studied for a Master's, wrote course and resource books, became a researcher at Lisbon's esteemed Nova University and specialised in interculturality and how it can improve students' language proficiency. Now she manages the triple roles of classroom teacher, project leader and mentor, an arrangement that she knows suits her energy and enthusiasm. She says she is not an extraordinary teacher but I beg to differ.

The junior secondary school Candida teaches at is in a deprived rural area on the outskirts of Porto, with around 1,200 students, 180 teachers and staff. There is a huge, vibrant local population of migrants and immigrants including people from Ukraine, Brazil, Venezuela and the Roma community, which creates a diverse classroom with mixed needs. On average, only three per cent of the students' fathers went to university, and five per cent of their mothers. Candida teaches from seventh grade (age eleven/twelve) to ninth grade (age fourteen/fifteen) before students leave to go to secondary school. Her English classes are popular because she takes a different approach to teaching.

'I nurture open-minded students and encourage strong opinions. I start every class with an activity that I call Spice Up. I raise a controversial issue, usually something in current affairs, and they discuss it between them. It is designed as a five-minute exercise, and if they get stuck I gently nudge them by throwing in a quote or an alternative point of view. It helps with critical awareness and enables them to use their own voice. They can be verbally fighting but also completely respecting the other's opinion, and they amaze me every time.'

Candida can see how confident her students become, and she is grateful that the school trusts and supports her methods. The benefits speak for themselves, particularly as many of the children come from difficult backgrounds and have complex needs, and a few have been removed from their family home and are in foster care. There is one girl Candida will never forget, who marked her as a teacher.

'Anna was my student in eighth grade. She was an incredibly calm, considered child but you could sense there was more to her story. She kept her arms concealed in long sleeves, but one day I glimpsed her skin and it was covered in marks so I asked her what had happened and she told me she didn't want to talk about it.'

Initially Candida thought she could have been self-harming or was covering up scars from a skin disease. Without Anna's willingness to speak, Candida became more attentive and careful around her, and eventually Anna confided in her.

'She told me everything about her life and I was devastated. When Anna was four years old her mother put her in a scalding-hot bath and her stepfather would stub out his cigarettes on her. She was regularly beaten. She was only saved because a wonderful neighbour took her in when she was six years old and had cared for her ever since. I was in tears listening to her story.'

At eleven, Anna navigated school with exceptional wisdom and understanding despite the early trauma she had experienced. She displayed an innate kindness and care towards her peers and would comfort those who were struggling and chastise those who misbehaved. She was a great influence on everyone she met.

'One of her friends, Pedro, was really naughty. He would do nasty things and she would tell him not to behave like a child and he listened to her.'

Anna's anger was reserved for only one person, her mother, who she hated.

Unsurprisingly, Anna had many learning difficulties, and Candida helped her progress to a vocational course at secondary school before she went on to take a degree in a professional course.

'She was such a brave girl. I am not sure she would have been alive if she hadn't been rescued. And she had such *joie de vivre*! It made me realise how lucky I was. Sure, I have had troubles and bad things happen in my life but really, what did I have to complain about? I learned the most from her, as a teacher and as a human being. She was a hero.'

Candida and Anna lost touch several years ago, but the last she knew Anna had moved away from Porto and was settled and happy.

'I am sure she is doing something that she likes. And she told me she wanted to have children so that she could be the mother to them that she never had. She will be a great mum.'

This story is both heartbreaking and heart-warming and I can see how much it has shaped the teacher Candida has become. She talks about being marked by some of her other students, and this feels irreversible and powerful. Like Daniel, who Candida first met when he was nine when he took part in a volunteering project she ran at Christmas. It involved the students collecting donations of food and presents that were then gifted to poorer households in the local community.

'I knew Daniel was different, he was so mature for his age. He was articulate and he worked very hard. He would always be asking if I needed anything or if he could help. Sadly, he was also a prime target for bullies but from the moment we connected, I became a safe haven for him.'

Daniel would seek Candida out at breaktimes, where she was often working at her desk in the school library. He was constantly teased because of the mature way he dressed and spoke – using rich vocabulary and uncommon words – and he would share how he felt with Candida.

'I told Daniel to believe in himself because, one day, he would have the chance to be the person he is. I said, don't change, don't be something you are not, just to have friends. One day they will see you for the amazing person you are.'

In seventh grade, Candida became Daniel's teacher and he was thrilled. It meant Candida could give more time to him and focus on the issues arising from the bully culture in the class.

The turning point for Daniel came when the class were celebrating Martin Luther King Day. Students were invited to be involved in whatever way they wanted, so some put together PowerPoint presentations and others brought films in. Daniel came to school dressed in a black suit and asked if he could present his work first.

'Daniel stood on his own at the front of the class and delivered Martin Luther King's famous "I Have a Dream" speech by heart. He had learned the whole thing in English and he shared it with passion and performance. Some of his peers started laughing so I just looked at them and they stopped and slowly began to engage with Daniel. And the moment he finished? Everyone clapped and shouted, "You rock, man!" He was superb.'

Finally, his friends understood who he was and they accepted him. Daniel is now seventeen and recently sent Candida a poem he had written in English, thanking her for always being there for him.

'I tell my students that I am not their mother, I am their teacher, but they can always rely on me. And that's what Daniel did.'

They are still in regular contact. I expect Candida to tell me Daniel is following a career in show-business after his stellar performance, but he wants to become a doctor and she believes he will achieve his dreams.

'Last year he was off school for a month after back surgery, so all the teachers and his friends rallied round to share the work with him so he could continue at home. I went to visit him and he was very happy. With his persistence and work ethic, he can be anything he wants to be.'

It's a huge responsibility for teachers to be a role model and a safety net, yet Candida embraces this, knowing she is the only hope for some of her students. For those children, she is the only adult they can trust. A couple of years ago she was tasked with the additional role of dealing with behavioural problems and disciplinary processes at the school.

'The days were full of drama because I knew I had to punish the offending students. Some transgressions were so serious, the punishment was unavoidable, but I hated doing it because these children had such difficult lives. Whenever a student misbehaves I think, "What has happened to this kid? Something must have to affect them in this way." Every kid has a story to tell, whether it's positive or negative, but they are not naturally evil. In one case, a student revealed he was being abused by his Scout leader, which we then dealt with.'

Candida spoke to her headmaster, Fernando, about how painful she found the reprimands and asked to have the responsibility removed. He understood how much she suffered from each student's story and valued her commitment to creating wonderful experiences for her pupils. I know exactly how she feels. It takes a certain type of person to deal with pastoral and safeguarding issues and I can become too emotional at times.

'You know, the one truth I have discovered about children? They need attention. I tell parents, it takes five minutes, just ask your kids what they did and listen to the answer. And show them affection too. I have seen kids with everything money can buy – smartphones, fashion, holidays – but they were tremendously unhappy because their parents ignore them.'

One student Candida taught, Susannah, was part of a large and wealthy family. Her mother was a doctor, studying for her PhD abroad, and her father was in politics. They were never around. She and her siblings were brought up by the housekeeper, who became a mother to them all, always rushing around taking one to football practice and another for swimming lessons.

'Susannah and her siblings had everything apart from the one thing they craved, attention from their parents. Her rebellious behaviour in class reflected this. She was rude to all the teachers and complained all the time, but what she was really saying was, "I need you to notice me." It doesn't mean a child is okay if they come from a wealthy background, they still have issues. Susannah liked English and so she liked me. When she left, she gave me a teddy bear wearing a heart that said, "I love you". It was reassuring that she could show affection and I hope she has found it for herself.'

Martin Salvetti

49, Buenos Aires, Argentina

'What makes me happy, and fills me with hope, is to see my students show empathy and care for each other'

Martin is the bedrock of his community. A teacher and mentor, he is also a public official in the municipal government. He had not considered a teaching career but he began tutoring at his childhood school in Buenos Aires to earn money to get him through university, and realised this was his destiny. He was barely older than the students he was teaching, in some cases only a year older. Twenty-eight years later he is still there.

'It is what I know how to do and I enjoy doing it. Teaching allows me to be part of the intellectual and emotional development of people . . . and that is what makes me happy.'

Temperley, the technical school where Martin works, has students from diverse and disadvantaged backgrounds who are learning vocational skills to combat the high level of youth unemployment in Argentina. Out of 1,600 children, only 250 of them are female, a higher figure than in previous years but still low, reflecting the attitude towards girls and technical education.

Martin has a unique approach to holding his students' attention. As a young teacher, he understood them and searched for ways to connect with them through learning. He established a school football club, uniting staff and students, which encouraged a mutually respectful and beneficial interaction. Martin also noted how focused the students were when they were active and part of a team experience, and this sowed the seed for the teacher he was to become.

Through Martin's role as Professor of Materials Knowledge, Technical Drawing and Internal Combustion Engines, he set up a collaboration between students from mechanics, metalworks and electronics to establish the 'A Car for a Horse' initiative. The project enables students to recycle motorbikes that have been seized by the city due to problems with documents, by attaching a cart to the motorbike. They then give them to deprived people who still use a horse and cart to collect recyclable rubbish from the streets. In turn, this also saves the horses from a life of cruelty.

Martin always connects his teaching to local and global issues, giving his students a much wider experience of the community and world around them. A perfect example of this was when he used arts programme funding to found a school radio station. A few years later, it won awards for the best education project in Argentina. Martin used the prize money to invest in equipment and a permit to be the first public-school radio station in the city. The debut transmission was in 2008 and it now broadcasts twenty-four hours a day, seven days a week, and is run entirely by the students.

'The radio station is not there to make them journalists. It's an educational tool. It also gives teachers the opportunity to evaluate their pupils in a different way from the traditional classroom.'

This approach is invaluable for many of the students, ninety per cent of whom need assisted learning. So too is the respect they have gained, not just from their teachers but from other local schools who regularly visit the radio station to learn from Martin's students. The broadcast content features entertainment, including poems and creative writing by the pupils, as well as covering important subjects like bullying, sex education, religion, children's rights and environmental issues. There have also been interviews with the human rights organisation Mothers of the Plaza de Mayo, which campaigns for those whose children were victims of forced disappearances over forty years ago.

'This is all about developing the students' sense of belonging and their vocation. They may not be the best at technology, but they are the best people. Like Sebastian.'

One of the students, fourteen-year-old Sebastian, asked Martin if he could work on the radio station. He wanted to take a presenting role but couldn't pronounce his 's's and struggled to read. He did not have learning difficulties but came from a background where he hadn't been encouraged or supported. He had never been given a book, so Martin sent him to the library and told him to pick something to read. He didn't expect what happened next.

'He read Kafka's *Metamorphosis* in three days! Within two months he had read seven books. He then asked me if he could interview an Argentinian journalist and historian, who himself was well known from an interview he had done in the past with Che Guevara. The interview was amazing – they talked about the Cuban Revolution.'

Sebastian had been studying electromechanics, but changed to history. The radio station had given him the confidence and ability to be who he wanted to be. Martin has created a place where all students have a voice and can show their potential in a way they couldn't in the classroom. He empowers the older students to teach the younger ones, which has helped them understand the role of the educator and, through this, one student discovered his vocation as a special needs teacher. Other careers have been established from Martin's mentoring, including a student who opened a motorbike repair shop and others who have gone on to work in the theatre and music industries.

'What makes me happy, and fills me with hope, is to see my students show empathy and care for each other. I see this in those who have gone on to become teachers themselves and who adopt my methods and philosophy to reach their class. For me, it's about meaningful learning and being taught skills they can take into their future.'

There are students who are difficult to help. Eight and six years ago, Andreas and Thomas struggled with drawing and, no matter how hard and how many ways Martin tried to work with them, they just couldn't do it. In both cases, he is still in touch with the boys, and they all joke about it now, but I know Martin feels he has let them down in some way. Of all the many children Martin has taught, it is these two that he reflects on. As an art teacher, I know how he feels. There are so many students who are fearful of drawing and who struggle, for many reasons, including with the confidence to translate a line into shape and form. Often students find it hard to see three-dimensional shapes and overlapping images.

Martin is keen to build relationships with parents, not just the pupils.

'I ask them to trust and value the teachers and the school because it's with that trust that we can do our best work. And to engage with their children on what they are doing at school and how they can support them at home. Each family needs to be part of the educative community. I know it can be hard for them because they come from diverse backgrounds, so we cannot expect the same from every parent.'

Martin is committed to striving for a better future for all, as both a teacher and a public servant. He isn't giving up, even though he admits that his goal may be impossible.

'We need to transform the education system in Argentina. And we need to lead our students to become the adults they were meant to be.'

Martin and I may not speak the same language, but we share the same outlook on education and our students. He refers to me as a 'lighthouse' but I know if anyone can make change happen, it will be Martin.

Marie Ghanbari

39, Muenster, Germany

'Go outside with your children and be physically active. That part of my childhood was the strongest, best side of me – when we ran, climbed trees and learned how to swim with my mum'

One of Marie's earliest memories is her experience of feeling judged. At primary school, a teacher labelled her incompetent. Marie was struggling with anxiety and low self-esteem at the time, as her parents were divorcing, and she failed to get into the junior high school she wanted to go to.

'The teacher had a big negative impact on me. It was a self-fulfilling prophecy and it took me a long time to shake off. My strengths were the support of my mum and the physical activity we did outside of school. And then I met a wonderful teacher, Ingrid, in Grade Eight, who became like a mentor to me. I wouldn't have done so well without her.'

Marie's confidence grew, as did her ability, and she began to find the fun in learning. She saw her own potential and this spurred her on to surpass her school's expectation. Marie gained her high school degree and took a gap year, going to New York to be an au pair.

'While I was in New York I took a college course in civil rights and victims and the law. When I returned to Germany I decided I wanted to study law because I wanted to fight for justice, not just in my country but in the world. I had huge optimism.'

At this point, Marie was twenty and had her whole life ahead of her, but she felt something holding her back. She knew her childhood experiences were subconsciously affecting her reactions and thoughts in certain situations. Instead of ignoring the problem she decided to do something about it, and went into therapy.

'The weight on my shoulders began to lift and I felt more and more powerful. I realised I could do anything if I believed in myself and I wanted to give every child the same opportunity. I swapped my law course because I knew, if I wanted to have a positive impact in the lives of children, I needed to start at the beginning of the causal chain. I started to study sports science, mathematics and intercultural psychology at the University of Muenster, to become a teacher.'

Marie is emotional about this turning point in her life. She could see the possibilities for children that were being missed and she knew she could make a difference. After graduating she was given the award for the best Master's thesis, and started her PhD before she became a teacher. She now works in a comprehensive school – which does not academically stream children and embraces students from all backgrounds – and also at a local university as a lecturer and researcher. It is a progressive learning experience focusing on emotional, social and empathetic competence.

'Our students are seen as individuals, with self-organised lessons, social emotional classes and physical activity programmes. There is fun in their learning and yet they know if they are struggling with something they can talk to their teachers. We are there for them. You can see confidence shining brightly in their eyes.'

One of the central values Marie and her colleagues teach is the importance of empathy. This reminds Marie of Ava, one of her students over five years ago. Ava had come from primary school with a bad report that highlighted her poor exam results and suggested she had learning disabilities. This reminded Marie of her own experiences.

'Ava was an incredibly positive child, full of empathy and fuelled by injustice. She was so intelligent. I just thought, wow, how could her primary teacher be so wrong? I put away the feedback from her school. This did not describe the child I saw.'

Ava and Marie talked about her previous school and how she had felt in lessons.

'She said she would be overwhelmingly stressed in exams and sort of black out. The teacher took that as a sign of incompetence and gave her parents negative feedback.'

At one point the primary school even tried to get Ava a special needs status. What they didn't understand was how Ava's anxiety around failure adversely affected her. Marie saw that immediately and under her care Ava relaxed and blossomed. The transformational moment for Ava came when she took her first exam.

'I reassured her and told her I would be there. We approach tests with transparency so Ava was prepared, she knew what was ahead and this also helped. She knew that we all believed in her and this empowered her to believe in herself.'

It is always an amazing moment when you see a student escape the vicious circle of negative belief and truly feel success is within their grasp. It changes everything for them.

'Ava started to feel like she was a good student. Her grades began to climb and she found the joy in learning. At parents' evening, she and her mother both cried because they had never had positive feedback.

They were so happy. Ava gained entry to high school and is planning to study law or psychology at university.'

I can see how much Marie cares about Ava, and I am not surprised by this wonderful outcome. Marie has not only worked with children in her own country but has been part of an education project with a Nigerian school. She first met Chinwendu in 2009 when she embarked on the pilot of what became a continuing initiative, returning again in 2011, 2012 and 2013 and staying for several months each time.

'Chinwendu was a good student. Without being part of a project like ours she would not have had the money or the support to realise her full potential. We were the motor behind her, sponsoring and mentoring her, and she ultimately achieved a Master's. She now works in marketing and communication.'

They talked a lot about Nigeria and the Igbo culture Chinwendu was brought up in. Marie was given the Nigerian name Ifeoma, meaning 'good thing'.

'I learned so much from her and the Igbo values around community, family and hospitality. Chinwendu visited me in Germany and I had just had my daughter, she was four months old. Chinwendu was wonderful to her and showed such great sensitivity. As a first-time mum I was nervous and uncertain but she reassured me. She was always smiling and seeing the positive in everything. Chinwendu taught me that it's okay just to be who we are.'

Marie remains in touch with both Ava and Chinwendu. She says going to university to learn to become a teacher is only the beginning, the theory of the profession. The truth is, it isn't until you are faced with a class of thirty students that you know what sort of teacher you are.

'It is about understanding each child, why they get angry and what their emotions are telling us. When I talk to university students now about teaching they always ask the same question: how do we really see each child in the class? I tell them it takes time and you have to invest in every child as a person, not just a student. They have to know you get them.'

As well as crediting her high school teacher for saving her, Marie also talks about her mum, who was a PE teacher and a 'lion' for her children. She would encourage Marie and her siblings to be outdoors and take part in sport as much as possible.

'I want to tell all parents to do the same. Go outside with your children and be physically active. That part of my childhood was the strongest, best side of me – when we ran, climbed trees and learned how to swim with my mum.'

Marie now runs social sports projects for socially deprived refugee students and children with different development opportunities. She knows how important these activities are and how few families can afford to pay for physical activity or know how to encourage their children in active free play.

'Some parents haven't learned how to ride a bike or swim, so they are less likely to teach their children. They may not have the money to buy their child a bike or sign them up for swimming lessons. Through my projects, I can create these possibilities for children and show them how exercise benefits their physical and emotional wellbeing. And team sports really matter. It's not about winning and losing, it's about rhythm and team spirit.'

What strikes me about Marie is her resilience to turn her negative childhood experience with a teacher into a positive, enabling her to be a better teacher and reach out to students who need her. It's wonderful to behold.

David Mitchell

47, Argyll and Bute, UK

'We have the most incredible young people in our community. Yes, there are challenges, but we need to give them a chance to blossom and try our best, as parents, to let our children find their own way. We can be in the background as their guiding star'

David is celebrating. Dunoon Grammar School in Argyll and Bute, where he has been headteacher since 2013, has been shortlisted for the globally renowned competition, 'World's Best School Prizes'. It is one of only four UK schools to be selected, and David is particularly thrilled because it has been recognised for the Community Collaboration Award. The community plays a big part in the development of the school and support of students and, in return, the school is actively involved in the local area. David can revel in the success, not just as the head of the school, but as a former pupil.

'I was born and raised in Dunoon and went to the grammar school, where I became head boy. My father was the technical design and technology teacher there. He was a wonderful man, who everyone talked so highly of, so they were the best footsteps in which to follow. After university, I taught the same subject as Dad in several different schools. I was so happy being in the classroom that I never thought I would become a headteacher. However, when the position came up in my old school I knew it was my dream job and I was lucky enough to get it. I have no intention of leaving any time soon. I love coming into work every day.'

Dunoon was a thriving peninsula town and a popular tourist

destination for day-trippers. When David was a schoolboy, there was also a large American military base operating there. When the base shut down and the Americans left, the community struggled with deprivation and a falling population. Yet, in the last few years, the town has seen a resurgence in people settling, driven in part by the incredible community projects established recently. David and the school are at the very heart of this.

'I am immensely proud of the school and everyone in it. It is a true reflection of the power of the community and the importance of treating young people as individuals.'

As well as the traditional secondary education structure, there is a hostel attached to the school for those students who live too far away to make the daily journey. In addition, a learning centre was set up for young people with severe and complex needs, with around thirty students benefiting from the outdoor classroom, garden and polytunnel.

'One of the greatest moments in my job is when I walk down the corridor every day and see those students with disabilities, blossoming in the space we have provided for them. When they smile, it makes such a difference to my day.'

At the beginning of his headship, there was a small group of boys at the school who impressed David with their commitment and attitude to learning. One of them, Callum, stood out particularly. He was incredibly shy but, over the years, David built a close relationship with him and would encourage him to talk. Callum grew into a confident young man.

'I saw Callum blossom in front of my eyes. We believed in him, and so he began to believe in himself, and the once reserved boy became house captain. He did a lot of charity work including challenging fundraisers and the activities extended into school. He and his friends shared this wonderful attitude, which made such a difference, not just to me, but to the school, because they created a joyful ethos that still lives on today.'

Callum went away to university and when he graduated he returned to his hometown to work for an IT company because he wanted to give back to the community who had nurtured him.

David is keen to point out that for all those success stories there have been other students who struggled. Like John, who was not interested in school. His behaviour was challenging, including wandering the corridors during class, being rude to the teachers and starting fights, even with his friends. He and David had a rocky relationship to begin with, as David tried to lay down ground rules and nothing worked.

'One day, when John was about fourteen, he behaved badly again, so I brought him into my office. I could see how much he was struggling, but I still did not know the root of the problem. We started to talk and bonded over football and golf. Within a short space of time I realised that he was severely dyslexic but had managed to get through primary school and a year or so of secondary education without anyone spotting this. I asked him what he wanted to do when he left school and he said he was keen to get onto a construction apprenticeship.'

David took a radical next step in his effort to support John. Rather than forcing him into a traditional learning environment, he decided to create the curriculum that would benefit John when he came to apply for apprenticeships. The programme was called Exite, which stood for 'exit into employment'.

'We put together a pathway to suit his needs, where he could do the subjects he was interested in. We included work placements, invited trainers into the school and supported him through qualifications in subjects like health and safety at work. When John left school he was ahead of the game. His work experience went so well he was offered an apprenticeship at the same company.'

This was an unusual, brilliant solution, but it needed financial and hands-on support. Luckily David had the trust of his staff and community partners, and they also worked closely with various organisations. The minimal costs were met by local resources and a proportion of the school budget.

'Whenever I bump into John on the street, he always thanks me, almost ten years later. He says I changed his life but he changed the school. He opened a door to what was to come. It wasn't just John who needed this programme, there were other young people in the school who could benefit from vocational courses that would not only lead to employment, but prevent so many of our young people leaving the local area. As a rural community on a peninsula, we sometimes get forgotten about and thirty-four of our staff come over by ferry every day. We need to find as many opportunities as possible for our students to encourage them to stay if they want to.'

David admits that creating bespoke curriculums has been hard to achieve and they don't always get it right, but they have to date delivered over fifty empowering skill-based courses.

'Every student can apply to take part, regardless of their abilities and background. Ronan, our head boy, with straight A grades, applied for one of our courses and got a placement on a local paper. His dream was to become a Formula One journalist and now he writes for a Formula One website.'

I know how rare and special it is for a school to be the heart and soul of a community. David has a huge amount of local support and, in turn, he gives back to the community by producing these amazing young people. The best example of this is yet to come.

'We are currently working on a dream project with the town, to regenerate the area and encourage tourism. The plans include zip wires and cable cars for access to the mountains. The committee who are working on it have huge faith in our school and have given us the opportunity to create a junior advisory board. It means our students are leading this project in their community. It's a big risk for the committee because they have invested heavily in a positive outcome, and it's a huge responsibility for us, but it's an amazing validation for the school and the young people.'

One of the biggest lessons David has learned is never to judge a child. All behaviour is communication and it can tell us a lot about each student.

'Teachers should always try to dig deeper and understand what each student may be experiencing away from school. I was reminded of this when I delivered lunch to our free school meal entitlement students during lockdown. It was the first time I had been to their homes. I didn't know how they lived and I saw first-hand how tough things were for them.'

Like me, David is a parent in education, which can be a difficult combination, particularly with his children studying at the school he heads. In situations involving students we can dive in and help everyone, but when it comes to our own children we hold back. It is hard for the children of teachers; nobody wants their mum or dad wading in.

But they still deal with the same issues as other students, including battling with their homework.

'I may be a teacher, but I do not have a secret formula for getting your child to do their homework. I know so many parents struggle with this, as I do too. What I would say is not to pile the pressure on your child, then they are more likely to accept your help. One of the best ways to support them is by practical means, helping them plan out their work so they tackle it a chunk at a time with regular breaks.'

David believes we should allow our children to make their own mistakes and let them learn from them, while being there to give guidance.

'We have the most incredible young people in our community. Yes, there are challenges, but we need to give them a chance to blossom and try our best, as parents, to let our children find their own way. We can be in the background as their guiding star.'

One of the directions David is keen for some of his students to go in is teaching. He has seen many amazing young people display a natural ability for this vocational pathway and he wants to encourage them.

'We need the teachers who are there for the children. One of my students, twelve-year-old Eilidh, is a brilliant swimmer. She asked if she could miss a lesson on Friday afternoons so she could support the learning centre students at their swimming class. She has shown such an aptitude for working with children and I want to fuel that passion. We need these brilliant young people to be the teachers of the future.'

With leaders like David in our schools, the future looks bright.

Conclusion

My indebted thanks to all the teachers who agreed to be part of this book and generously shared their experiences. I am so grateful for their remarkable insights and poignant memories, which have often made me cry for happy and sad reasons. They display a passion for their profession that stretches way beyond their job title and defines who they are, and they make the students – not the curriculum, budget and assessments – their priority and cause for celebration. In sharing the truths they have absorbed from the students they have taught, we can also benefit.

So, what have you learned from these wonderful teachers? I can imagine you are as moved and inspired as I am by incredible young people overcoming adversity. I now challenge you to reflect on these stories, carry them in your daily life and try those ideas which are appropriate to your circumstances. Dip back into the essays whenever you need to. They may also have reminded you of your own positive experiences with teachers from your past who you are thankful for. There is so much wisdom among these pages that can support us all, whether we are parents, teachers or just navigating our way through life.

You have met just thirty extraordinary teachers, but they are everywhere, being quietly brilliant. I think this has been more evident during the pandemic, when children were home-schooled. I have a quote stuck on my noticeboard, origin unknown, that reads, 'Engineers make bridges. Artists make paintings. Scientists make rockets. But teachers make them all.'

Thank you to every teacher around the world, many working in very difficult conditions and never fully realising the impact they have on their community. I see you.

Acknowledgements

Firstly, my heartfelt thanks to Lucy Brazier, whose artistic genius made the conversations come to life. I really miss our Zoom chats and the sounds from your garden.

To my thirty magnificent friends who have given me permission to share their stories and for allowing me to step into their school worlds. Thank you for your patience and time, it was truly an honour to work with you.

Thank you to my wonderful editor Katy Follain, whose idea made this journey possible, and for her positivity and patience.

A huge thanks to the rest of the Quercus team: Nina Sandelson, Tania Wilde, Emily Patience, Andrew Smith, Jon Butler, Lipfon Tang, David Murphy, Chris Keith-Wright, Emma Thawley, Hannah Cawse, Ian Binnie, Jacqui Lewis and Rhian McKay.

To my wonderful agent Rachel Mills, thank you for your energy, support and for always being there.

To my team at Artists in Residence: George and Joe, thank you for your support and dedication.

To Vikas for your support and for always taking my calls twenty-four hours seven days a week.

I am fortunate for the love and encouragement I receive from my friends, parents and siblings for the work that I do – thank you.

Finally, to my always patient husband John, my daughters Sophia and Anna Maria, for lifting my spirit, the endless cups of tea, and for putting up with me.